IN SEARCH OF
BALANCE:

Rediscovering Simple Christianity

**This is the first edition book.
The newest edition
"Finding Your Spiritual Balance in a
Religious World: Discovering Simple
Christianity" is now available on
Amazon and other E-book sites.**

BY

KENNETH L. WEATHERFORD

xulon PRESS

TABLE OF CONTENTS

Acknowledgments

———

I want, particularly, to thank a young British man who understood the Christian Walk far better than any modern person I've ever met. I only know of him through what he taught and his wife wrote down. As a young man, he began and operated a school for missionaries at which he taught some of the most wonderfully simple and insightful truths about what it really means to be a Christian. He died a young man while in His Majesty's service (both secularly and spiritually) as a chaplain to British troops at the Suez Canal in World War I. Thankfully, his wife wrote down virtually all of his lessons and transcribed them into a book we know now as *My Utmost for His Highest*. This was Oswald Chambers. After over 40 years of being a follower of Jesus the Messiah, I continue to be amazed at the godly wisdom of this incredible man. I've read and reread this book for many years now.

I want, also, to thank those legalistic traditionalists who, over the years, wished to burden me (and many others) down with rules and regulations—none of which Jesus started—to where like onto themselves a "joyful" smile resembled more of a grimace of pain. Also, those fomenters of "relevant religion" in which the primary focus of everything in their ministry becomes to throw out all traditions and structure and set up a new order of anti-rules and anti-traditions in order to be "relevant" to the society around them. I love them all despite their dislike of my stand, but they have inspired me to finally write this book.

Relevancy and diversity seem to be the "catchwords" of society today, but Jesus did not strive for being relevant to the society around Him. If He had strove to be relevant He would have worked to become a Pharisee instead of rebuking them for their callousness toward the people. Jesus definitely believed in spiritual diversity. His message, of necessity, was initially to the lost sheep of Israel, but He ministered to Samaritans, a Phoenician woman and a Roman centurion to name just a few. The Samaritan (half-Jews and idolaters) village of Sychar where He ministered for a few days was actually the first people group to declare that He was the Messiah. Jesus broke the religious mold, but that was exactly what He came to do.

If He had been relevant in that extremely "religious" society, He wouldn't have done what He came to do—set us free from that stuff! That is my hope for this book—to set free and/or keep free those who call on the name of Jesus of Nazareth, the promised Messiah of the Old Testament. There is a reason totalitarian governments hate Christianity. It "sets the captives free." It, in its true form, creates freedom and liberty. Our own nation, the United States of America, was founded on those principles and guess where they came from–our founding fathers who were mostly Christians, many of whom were ordained ministers. Unfortunately, there are those among the ranks that want to stifle freedom and return to rules and laws. That is not freedom; that is bondage. Jesus freed us from bondage. Don't be like the Israelites leaving Egypt, always tempted to go back to slavery!

There are several others I must thank. One, my wife of over 40 years who swam the turbulent sea of religion with me in quest of the real Christian Walk; she has been a constant encourager to (one day) get this on paper. And, two, I thank my pastor and friend, Pastor Tim Stevens, of Azle First Assembly of God, Azle, Texas, for his encouragement. I knew I'd found the right church and pastor when, in one of the first sermons I heard from him, he said the very important statement (to me) of "there is balance in the Word of God." I'd been urging church people for a decade about the need for balance, staying away from the extremes, the "rabbit trails" and the "pop-Christian" versions of Biblical promises in order to focus on Jesus. I've found a real spiritual home at his church and a lot of real Christian friends who also encourage me. Much thanks to them also! And I want to thank those folks like Chris Yeargan and my oldest son, Ross, who took time from busy schedules and boisterous active sons to check my chapters for flaws and readability. Thanks to all!

PREFACE

———⦿———

The Church is Waking-up Again! Do You Want to be Part of That?

I do not pretend to be a great theologian or a Biblical scholar. I am a non-or-dained lay person, a simple believer in Jesus Christ. (By the way, Jesus and His Apostles were not ordained either. Ordained is good, but not required in order to be a Christ follower, teacher, or leader.) However, He has given me a desire to put things of His kingdom's nature down on paper in a simple, balanced way. Many people have made it seem very complicated and unbalanced. The Oswald Chambers and A. W. Tozer's of Christian history have tried to keep the train on the tracks along with many others, but others—intentionally or not — keep trying to derail it.

There are many people, today, seeking and finding the Christianity of Jesus of Nazareth despite the all the disinformation (intentional or not) of some leaders, teachers and writers. We are in the third generation after the last spiritual renewal of the 60s to 70s known vicariously as the "Charismatic Renewal." These renewals, known also as Great Awakenings, happen approximately every 3 generations or about 50 or so years. Some "experts" refuse to call the Charismatic Renewal the last Great Awakening. Apparently they were not paying attention or weren't born yet, for those of us who experienced it, it was real. Very real indeed! And it had the usual ripple effects upon the society in general that real awakenings always have over the centuries.

Like then, churches are once again dropping their denominational titles and taking on names that more identify them with the early church of the Bible when there were no Baptists, Methodists, Lutherans, Assemblies of God, Catholic, etc. groupings. There is nothing wrong, per se, with being denominational as long as a group follows the Word of God, the Bible, for its doctrine. It is just that, now, many people want to identify directly with what they are learning from the Word! (For much of the rest of the book, I prefer to refer to the "Bible" as "the Word" as in Word of God.)

Grammar

Perhaps because of the adaption of word processing and electronic spell checking (or English teachers taking over), most translations now do not capitalize pronouns or other words used in place of members of the Godhead (Trinity). Please do not be confused as you read the book. Most of the scripture references inserted into the text do not capitalize these. I do in my text. It is what is called a "personal conviction" in that I don't feel comfortable not capitalizing them. It is not a sin to not capitalize them. It is just that I feel more comfortable emphasizing God's high office no matter what pronoun or descriptive I'm using for Him or an attribute of Him. In some Bible passages, it can also get confusing who the he or him is without capitalization of God's pronouns!

Why I Finally Wrote the Balance Book

For many years, I've been journaling, writing articles, devotions, lessons on what I call "The Balanced Gospel" as opposed to all the "rabbit trails" people go off onto for various reasons. I've always wanted to put it into a book that would hopefully help all those who are looking for the middle ground in their Christian walk. This middle ground is not safe and comfortable for there is no such thing if you are a Christ-follower, just middle as in solid, un-potholed center of the road. My hope and prayer is that the book will help steady those who are really interested in what Jesus actually did for us and teaches us. And, I hope it is an aid for those who do not want to be constantly distracted from the path He set for us. The Gospel is very simple, but to many it has become too complicated and even unbearable by man's interventions.

A primary personal reason for this book is that, unfortunately, most new Christians or those investigating Christianity do not get mentored on how to relate all the information concerning various doctrinal and non-doctrinal issues covered in the Bible. (Contrary to some "opinions," not every word in the Bible is a rule or law we have to follow!) I went through this and many times, it was years before I was able to sort out various doctrinal (and non-doctrinal) topics in the Word. Biblical information is not necessarily in chronological order and, often, one must search through other books of the Bible for related material to fill in the gaps. There are often some substantial gaps in time between what is recorded.

I'm not saying that I am the perfect mentor myself (I am a teacher and love teaching), but what I am attempting to do is to place scripture and comments in a more logical trail for a student's comprehension. In some cases, what I had been taught by very well-meaning and respected mentors I later found to be "religiously" biased by traditional (man-sanctioned) interpretations. Throughout the book, my intention is to avoid "religion" and stick with what the Word, itself, says. If I seem to you to fail in that, please forgive me.

Chapter One

THE NEED FOR BALANCE

———∞∞∞———

My First "Christian" Religious Experience

Back in the 50s when I was a young boy of perhaps 6, an adult relative took me one moonless night to a "revival service" that her "pastor" was having somewhere out in the country. (The slang word "boondocks" would be more appropriate.) This relative in her late teenage years had been suddenly caught up with a "Christian" group who seemed very secretive and very conservative. Some of them even took on really melodramatic names like "Morningstar." (In the New Testament, this refers to Jesus Christ. In the Old Testament in the book of Isaiah it refers to Satan as an archangel before his fall from grace and his eviction from Heaven.) I remember that it was an extremely dark night, but what awaited this (not so) innocent pre-elementary boy was something more dark and terrifying than any 1950s horror movie he'd seen, or even some pretty scary Alfred Hitchcock shows that he had watched while hiding behind the bed at home.

In the middle of a very dark and lonely field on this pitch black night, seemingly in the middle of absolute nowhere, there was a semi-tumbled down shack that reverberated with the screams, agonies and yells of "worshippers" with some "preacher" ranting, raving and screaming at them at the top of his voice. There must have been 20 to 30 "worshippers" but the "preacher" was just about the only man there. What little light there was came from kerosene lanterns placed here and there in the ramshackle rooms within. Many of the worshippers were screaming at the top of their lungs as if the devil himself were tearing their guts out in various positions from kneeling to rolling on the floor to throwing themselves about! To a six year old child it was total and terrifying chaos! It should have been rated XXX for children just for the terror factor.

My relative wanted to leave me in that mayhem while she became one of the unmedicated inmates in the ward. I don't remember exactly how it transpired, but I think she finally realized that if she didn't take me home, I'd be running as fast as my child-sized legs could move in whatever direction took me away from this version of hell as I thought it! I was utterly terrified. Hell, in my mind, could not have been worse! Many years later, she admitted to me that this and several of the outfits she belonged to during that early period were shams–phony "churches" to take advantage of people by some itinerant "preacher."

But the damage was done. It was not until many years later when I read a Bible of my own in my own language that I realized that God did indeed give various spiritual gifts to the church in order for it to flourish, to serve as a sign to believers and unbelievers, and to provide for the financial and physical health of believers. But the utter chaos and bizarre scary behavior I had been exposed to at an early age I did not find anywhere in the Word of God (the Bible).

Until I found out what the real church of the Bible was, I kept my distance from any church or group that used the name "Pentecostal", "Full-Gospel", or anything similar. Descriptive terms such as these were good in the beginning and still good among those keeping the right perspective. Unfortunately, they can and do take on a "life of their own" religiously in the minds of those who have been negatively conditioned by the media or by bad teaching or been traumatized by the excesses of some groups. Such as, a small church out in the country where you would find yourself among people handling rattlesnakes and other poisonous critters as part of the service. This is actually done by some small isolated groups and is "justified" by taking out of context and misusing the verse Luke 10:19 in which Jesus tells his 72 disciples as He is sending them out to evangelize: "[19]Behold, I give unto you power to tread on serpents and scorpions, and over all the power of the enemy: and nothing shall by any means hurt you" (KJV).

He was not telling His disciples to go out of their way to find poisonous animals to step on and to handle! He did not say that a Christian had to prove their faith by this kind of behavior or any other particular kind of behavior. Matthew, in his Gospel describing Jesus's temptations, stated, "⁵Then the devil took him to the holy city, Jerusalem, to the highest point of the Temple, ⁶and said, "If you are the Son of God, jump off! For the Scriptures say, 'He will order his angels to protect you. And they will hold you up with their hands so you won't even hurt your foot on a stone.'" ⁷Jesus responded, "The Scriptures also say, '*You must not test* [my italics] the LORD your God'" (Matthew 4:5-7, NLT).

Jesus was telling His disciples they would have the protection of the Holy Spirit. For example, years later the Apostle Paul had a poisonous viper latch onto his hand on the island of Malta. He shook it off and didn't swell up and die, much to the amazement of the natives whom he then had the opportunity to evangelize. (I don't recommend you try this for street evangelism!) This is what Jesus was talking about–protecting His believers. To "test" God (some versions use "tempt") can show a lack of faith on the individual's part and a lack of respect for God. I say "can" because there is a biblical example of "testing" God (read Judges 6:33-40). In those passages, no Israelite had heard from God in a long time and, suddenly, a Jewish man named Gideon was being asked by "God" to fight a huge army with a paltry few Israelites. In the same situation, I would probably ask for "proof" like he did. But that had nothing to do with New Testament salvation. God sacrificed His son for that "snake handler's" salvation. It is not necessary to "prove" our faith to God! Jesus made it possible for God to know our hearts. He already knows our faith!

In studies some years ago, I came across something that the historically famous "Father of International Law" Hugo de Grotius said, who was an ardent Christian and paid for it with imprisonment and exile. It applied, in his day and now, to relationships between nations and it applies to the promotion of Christianity. In addressing the problem with self-righteous people fanning the flames of the religious war fervor between the Catholic and Protestant churches in Europe, he said, "But I think they have followed the familiar practice of going from one *extreme* to the other in the pursuit of truth. This attempt to go too far in the other direction often causes more harm than good, since *their extremism in one area loses them respect as far as their more reasonable claims are concerned* [my italics]. We should therefore remedy their arguments, so that people are not encouraged to believe either nothing or everything that they say."[i]

We see the same problem in promoting Christianity to others today. The national media only presents extremists and radicals to the general public. Television series and movies (not all) present Christians as ignorant, insensitive bigots; and, unfortunately, within our ranks (or at least some who claim to be in our ranks) we have "religious" bigots who seem to enjoy going around offending everyone they meet! In our current time, we have a small group from a southeastern state that publicly burns the holy book of another religion to inflame that group's follower's hatred for "Christians" and Americans in general. That is extremism. Another small inbred group from "up north" rudely interrupts funerals of men and women who have died in combat for their nation. These are extremists. Their behavior is not acceptable and NOT Christian. If Jesus cries in Heaven, He is crying over the horrible false image of His people that these types of people promote through the mainstream media.

These extremists and others plus our own very human "opinionated" out-bursts sometimes, can negate anything a non-believer hears that is truth. So, what do we do (or you do if you are looking at Christianity)? So how do we Christians, as de Grotius says it, "…remedy their arguments, so that people are not encouraged to believe either nothing or everything that they say?"[ii] How? We need to stay centered on our relationship to Jesus Christ and not get off on legalistic and extreme political tangents that take our (and our observer's) eyes off of Him. A person's personal relationship with Jesus is what it is all about, not "grandstanding" for the media. Public debate is good and voting for your candidate is your right, but Christians need to avoid being manipulated and used by politicians and pundits. We belong to Christ, not a political boss.

To quote the Apostle Paul in his first letter to the Corinthian Church, "¹Dear brothers and sisters, when I came to you, I did not come preaching God's secret with fancy words or a show of human wisdom. ²I decided that while I was with you I would forget about everything except Jesus Christ and his death on the cross" (1 Corinthians 2:1-2, NCV). Other translations simply say "Christ and Him crucified…." He preached the "core value" of Christianity to the Corinthians. *Jesus death on the cross was the fulcrum, the balance point of all history and the central issue of Christianity itself.*

We may be a Baptist, Methodist, Assembly of God, Catholic, Lutheran or belong to any number of Christian denominations, but primarily we must individually be a Jesus-following and loving Christian. We cannot help anyone accept Jesus if all they see are people squabbling over what is mostly "personal convictions" not real sin! I'll address "personal convictions" versus sin in the chapter on "Trial, Temptation, or Sin." Basically, if someone believes something is a sin that is not identified as a sin in scripture, it is a sin for them only (see Romans 14).

The Apostle Paul in his evangelistic travels throughout the Middle East and parts of what is now known as Europe adapted to the culture and didn't argue about "side issues." He stated it this way, "²⁰To the Jews I became like a Jew, to win the Jews. To those under the law I became like one under the law (though I myself am not under the law), so as to win those under the law. ²¹To those not having the law I became like one not having the law (though I am not free from God's law but am under Christ's law), so as to win those not having the law. ²²To the weak I became weak, to win the weak. I have become all things to all people so that by all possible means I might save some" (1 Corinthians 9:20-22, NIV).

If you compare these verses with other Bible translations, you will find that he emphasizes that he adapts to the culture, but is always under the law of Christ. In other words, he adapted to the culture and honored their customs, but did not do anything or honor/practice a custom that would violate his faith in Jesus. Christians are emissaries of Jesus Christ not promoters of the "American

Dream," capitalism, democracy, republican, democrat, "tea party," or any such thing. Patriotism for your nation is fine, but our *first allegiance is to God.*

American Christian missionaries have been known to teach American customs of dress, manners and other things to converts as if these were Christian virtues. I feel certain that missionaries from other nations have many times done the same thing. To keep things in balance we need to keep in mind what Christ said about how we must live, not our local customs, traditions, or manner of government. When someone becomes a follower of Christ, they are supposed to "rise" above worldly things.

When my walk with Jesus began shortly after reading the Living Bible in my early twenties and recommitting my life to Him, the first scripture that the Holy Spirit emphasized to me was in Jesus's Sermon on the Mount. I needed it because I was "self-made" and self-reliant. I didn't trust anyone to supply my needs except me! This part of His sermon could not have been more appropriate for the renewal of my walk. Here is what He said:

[24]"No one can serve two masters. For you will hate one and love the other; you will be devoted to one and despise the other. You cannot serve both God and money.[25] That is why I tell you not to worry about everyday life—whether you have enough food and drink, or enough clothes to wear. Isn't life more than food, [*sic*] and your body more than clothing? [26] Look at the birds. They don't plant or harvest or store food in barns, for your heavenly Father feeds them. And aren't you far more valuable to him than they are? [27] Can all your worries add a single moment to your life? [28] And why worry about your clothing? Look at the lilies of the field and how they grow. They don't work or make their clothing, [29] yet Solomon in all his glory was not dressed as beautifully as they are. [30] And if God cares so wonderfully for wildflowers that are here today and thrown into the fire tomorrow, he will certainly care for you. Why do you have so little faith? [31] "So

don't worry about these things, saying, 'What will we eat? What will we drink? What will we wear?' [32] These things dominate the thoughts of unbelievers, but your heavenly Father already knows all your needs. [33] Seek the Kingdom of God above all else, and live righteously, and he will give you everything you need. [34] So don't worry about tomorrow, for tomorrow will bring its own worries. Today's trouble is enough for today" (Matthew 6:24-34, NLT).

This was a revelation for me because I was a worrier, had a lot of anger and frustration and had no concept of being "carefree" in God. I was not "Christ-centered," I was "me-centered." I was way "off balance." I was following the American ideal of the self-made, self-reliant man and it was eating me alive!

Like Paul, though, you and I must still honor those customs of our society or the one we are visiting as long as it doesn't violate the law of Christ. The "Law of Christ" is higher than any human written law. This is where the conflict comes frequently between societies/government and real Christianity. At one time in America, this was not a problem. Things are changing; but we are not supposed to worry about tomorrow.

The Holy Spirit Will Guide You into the Right Path

As I was to find out as an adult, reborn Christian, and student of the Word, God was a God of gentleness, love, forgiveness, and companionship–not a purveyor of bizarreness, terror, chaos, or fear (unless you were the enemy of God-fearing Hebrews of the Old Covenant). Some "strange" things historically and contemporarily happen to people who encounter God in the form of His Son Jesus, but not scary stuff. But along the way, I found there were other extremes. Legalism is the opposite of emotionalism in the broad interpretation of Christianity. (Although, there often is a "legalistic expectation" that creates the atmosphere for extreme emotional behavior or "hyper-spirituality" as some call it.)

In my personal experience with legalism, there was no screaming, yelling, or rolling on the floor; instead, there was quietly mumbled prayers said very carefully so as not to sound like heresy. Worship of the words of the Bible instead of the Word of God (Jesus) to the same level of heresy of the Pharisees of Jesus time. They, like the Pharisees, took the words meant to keep peoples' minds on God to be gods themselves, to take and extrapolate those simple words into additional "books of laws" to heap, as Jesus called them, burdens upon people's backs that even the perpetrators could not bear. That is called "dead religion!" There is no life in it for Jesus is not there in their "midst." (See Matthew 18:20.)

However, on an individual basis you could be like I was–frequently as we studied the Pharisees or similar legalistic Biblical types, this small voice in my mind would say (with emphasis), "You are studying yourselves!" Fortunately, I had my salvation experience many years before and even though I drifted away and then for a while was in legalism, the Holy Spirit did not leave me and was just reminding me. I didn't want to admit it at the time, but I knew Who it was! That is where one can say truthfully, "God is good!" Eventually, He encouraged me out of legalism and back into a "real" church.

If you study the Word in your language, comparing translations and calling on God to give you better comprehension through the intercession of the Holy Spirit of God, you will find that the Word of God (the Bible) is a document that is "balanced" in its information and its approach. Unfortunately and frequently, mankind does not do it the justice of reading it that way. They read it with an agenda or prior expectations or just simply believe what they are told by intentional or unintentional deceivers.

Deceit and Deceivers Are Nothing New!

Jesus and His Apostles and many other writers in the Bible warned that there were not only already deceivers in the early church, but it would continue to be so until the end of time. There would and will always be people claiming to be

Christian, and perhaps some were at one time, who bring disgrace upon Jesus's name and the church by openly and intentionally practicing deceit. We in Jesus Church do not confuse these people with "Christianity", but the media and the world at large do. As with the earlier examples, the media will pick up on one or two small condemnation-filled groups that call themselves "Christians" and tout these as if they represented the real followers of Jesus Christ. These are what they use for their stereotypical "fundamentalists." It is up to us Christians to show them the way it really is. That is what this book is about–what really being a Christian is about. What are the basics a Christian believes? Where is the balance that is missing?

There are all kinds of ways that men and women, intentionally and unintentionally, pervert the Word of God to suit themselves, to enslave others, to make life more unbearable than it already can be, or simply because they do not comprehend scripture. Many of them are well-meaning or just plain wrongly taught. The great Apostle Paul, who evangelized much of the Roman non-Jewish world, was once a highly educated Pharisee who knew the Old Testament histories and Law completely and should have known who Jesus was by the prophecies he knew by heart. Instead, because of what he was taught, he persecuted Christians (even to the death) until he met up with the resurrected Jesus one day. So, forgive those who wrongly teach the Word (even the intentional ones) as dead religion and pray for them to change. Pray for them to meet the real Jesus as Paul did.

God's Word is meant to make our lives more bearable, not less! It is meant to give us life, not death; it is meant to free us, not enslave us! Many years ago, I came across a saying which I use to this day–"Religion is the way man tries to control God (and men). Relationship is what God wants with man."

I believe that we Western Civilization-type people (the heritage of Greek philosophy and thinking) have a strong tendency to categorize everything possible. There are some of us who are really bad about this–very analytical. I'm one and have to be very careful. People take the Word of God, analyze it, categorize it, sanitize it, legalize it and, as a result, euthanize it! It becomes merely dead religion or masses of rules that followers numb their minds and their hearts to God while trying to follow and please Him by their adherence to, mostly, man-made rules. That is not Christianity! That is death!

Unfortunately, anytime there is a legitimate move of God, often referred to as "awakenings" there come the devil's counterfeiters also. Some are con artists, some are mentally "driven" and some really believe what they preach, but they ruin a lot of people and serve as rallying points for anti-Christians as in Sinclair Lewis's book, *Elmer Gantry* (1926) which was made into a movie in 1960. Fortunately, by God's grace, some of these exploited people are able to recover as with the relative that drug that 6-year-old boy to a "revival," but many may never set foot in a church again! (Actually, you do not have to go into a church to be saved; God is bigger than buildings!)

Today, those who try to rally sentiment against Christianity, use these examples, the Elmer Gantry's and other "fundamentalists" (fundamental does not mean the same thing to the mainstream media [MSM] that it does to Bible believers) to promote the idea that Christians are a bunch of ignorant bigots. Wake up, pay attention, and you will see how prevalent it has become on television and in movies! They carefully insert quick "digs" here and there portraying Christians or citizens of overall conservative states as insensitive, deceitful, or just plain ignorant.

The media and special interest groups often refer to Christians as "haters" these days. This stigmatization is only directed at Christians and rarely at other faiths. Christians aren't known (except for a few fringe types in the anti-abortion movement some years ago) for striking back. As Christians, we are forbidden from taking revenge on people who assail us (revenge, not self-defense). *This is a huge difference from many religions*. The "hater" title is directly in reference to those Christians who have condemning attitudes. We do have some Christians, though they say they "hate the sin and love the sinner" whose everyday words and behavior negate what they say. This is a quite human foible we all need to avoid whether we serve Jesus Christ or not! We have all failed in this area at one time or another if we are human. It is too easy to be condemning!

Likewise, the use of political correctness is really bad. It is a subtle form of condemnation. It borders on and can be the precursor to mind and thought control and strives to punish noncompliant people with termination of their jobs and other similar "punishments." However, much of what is "politically correct" is the same message Christianity is supposed to espouse–toleration of people who have a different opinion, compassion instead of condemnation, and not ridiculing people because of their differences. *These are things Christians should practice anyway.* Making fun of people is just another form of disguised condemnation hiding behind humor.

Real Christianity, though, does not try to force things on people. State religions do and have, whether they call themselves Christian or are another religion entirely. That is, again, why in the USA, our founding fathers banned having a state religion. Most of our early American immigrants came here to get away from being told what their religious beliefs would be and punished (or burned at the stake literally) if they didn't agree to convert.

Our current world is full of hatred and condemnation. Just look at the nightly line up on television today. Many of the favorite serials in prime time are based upon getting revenge or similar motivations. **Condemnation and revenge are not part of the Christian package!** Paul, in the Roman letter, said this, "[19] Dearly beloved, avenge not yourselves, but rather give place unto wrath: for it is written, Vengeance is mine; I will repay, saith the Lord" (Romans 12:19, KJV). I like the way the KJV says it. It is more forceful.

A sincere student of the Bible finds that Christians neither live under condemnation (as some legalists believe) nor are they to be condemners of others. In other words, they are not to be "haters" of anyone, even their enemies! When Jesus was, once again, being grilled by the Pharisees to try to get Him to say something the religious police (themselves) could arrest Him for, this is what happened:

> [36] "Teacher, what is the greatest commandment in the Law?" [37] He replied, "You must love the Lord your God with all your heart, with all your being, and with all your mind. [38] This is the first and greatest commandment. [39] And the second is like it: You must love

your neighbor as you love yourself. [40] All the Law and the Prophets depend on these two commands" (Matthew 22:36-40, CEB).

Love is the basic ingredient of Christianity. Hatred is not even in the same solar system except in Hollywood's or the mainstream media's normal version of Christianity. But since hatred and revenge seeking are all around us, it is an easy "pit" to fall into, so beware!

So What is Balance?

We live in an era when simple is not enough; although we know that complexity tends to confuse and frustrate us. It started with VCRs that had way more functions than anybody knew how to use or did. Then came the other electronic marvels (of which many I use) that still have way too much fun but unnecessary "bells and whistles." Unfortunately, mankind's approach to a relationship with his Creator suffers from the same malady. People now think that if it isn't multi-functional and they don't have to be multi-taskers; it can't possibly be the "right" thing. How could God simply want us to simply accept that He loves us and act on that? Doesn't it require a lot of razzle-dazzle, commotion, big speakers (both kinds) and resplendent facilities seating thousands? As a matter of fact–no! All that is required is for us as individuals to relate to our Creator and Savior.

Balance is many things to many people and applies to many different things, but is, essentially, the same in all cases. In an older autopilot system for an aircraft, it was based around a gyroscope, a spinning device in the control system that resisted any change to direction from straight and level. To a human or animal, but especially for bi-pedal humans, it is directed from the inner ear where "semi-circular canals" in the inner ears detect any movement away from the balance the person has achieved and help the animal or human correct their balance.

An example most people are familiar with is a seesaw or teeter-totter. If set up properly, it is in balance when finished; if used, we know that people of equal size or weight can sit on the seats at the ends and be in balance enough to move each other up and down with ease; if one is larger, they have to move closer to the "fulcrum" in order to be in balance with the other person. The fulcrum or pivot point is where the seesaw is attached and what the whole contraption teeters about. The fulcrum is the balance point and if the seesaw is not attached properly at that exact point, it won't work properly.

The gyroscope in the autopilot, the semi-circular canals in a human, the fulcrum on the seesaw all serve to keep things working the way they are meant to work. Without the gyroscope the plane could go out of control and crash. Without the semicircular canals, humans and animals would be flopping around on the ground instead of standing and walking. Without the fulcrum/pivot point the seesaw would merely slide off the beam, get people hurt and be worthless. Balance is important and there is normally some mechanism, an organ or device that is designed to maintain that balance.

Balance in the Gospel had been on my mind and frequently in things I wrote for the past decade when, upon visiting a new church, I heard the pastor state that there was "balance in the Gospel!" I knew that I'd finally found the right church. So, what do I (and he) mean by "balance in the Gospel?" It simply means that, just as in all of nature and mechanics, there has to be a force or "mechanism" that is central to the proper functioning of whatever system we are dealing with. To move away from that force, that central point of balance is to bring chaos, confusion, frustration or disaster. *Jesus's life, death and resurrection are absolutely central to Christianity. The crucifixion is the fulcrum.*

In summary, then what is the "balance point" in what we believe in Christianity? Paul said to the Corinthians, "²I had made up my mind not to think about anything while I was with you except Jesus Christ and to preach him as crucified" (1 Corinthians 2:2, CEB). He is talking about what he was going to teach about. *The Message*, returning to the original intent of the language, says this, "2 ¹⁻² You'll remember, friends, that when I first came to you to let you in on God's master stroke, I didn't try to impress you with polished speeches and the latest philosophy. I deliberately kept it plain and simple: first Jesus and who he is; then Jesus and what he did—Jesus crucified" (1 Corinthians 2:2, MSG).

Jesus's death and resurrection enabled your current or potential personal relationship with God through His Son, Jesus, with the Holy Spirit as your Guide. That is the balance point. Everything else spins off this.

Chapter Two

THE CHRISTIAN WALK

———❦———

Where are we–you and I? Is life treating us well? Are we getting out of life what we expected to achieve? Do we even know what we want to achieve or receive? What are our choices? Good or bad? Are our choices that simple? I felt inspired to write this poem a number of years ago for a special service. To me, it says it all.

THE GATE

There are two worlds really,
They exist side-by-side separated only by a small, easily traversed fence.
These are the physical world, in which we dwell, and the Supernatural.
The Supernatural world is divided into two realms–the Eternal, in which God dwells, in which there is everlasting peace, joy, and love
And the other, the Infernal, in which there is only unending darkness and despair, where God's presence is eternally missing.
Our present world is a meadow encircled by the fence.
In the fence are two opposing gates.
The gate to the infernal realm is wide with a well-paved path.
It remains always open, gaily decorated and inviting to all who

come close. Neon lights point the way and loud boisterous music and actors hail the virtues of this pathway. The pathway is easy to walk for it always leads gently downhill.

The gate to the Eternal is much more narrow. The path to it is not paved, but is cushioned by the brown dead leaves of worry and care cast off by former travelers. It winds gently uphill among small vales of beautiful wildflowers and through the refreshing shade of towering, majestic oaks. The non-pretentious white picket gate is closed, but opens at the slightest touch, for its hinges were lubricated long ago by the Blood of the Lamb of God – Jesus the Messiah. There is no neon, no noisome, cacophonous music, only a gentle soothing breeze, carrying fragrances of unearthly peace, unending joy, and unconditional love.

Many journey most of the way to this gate, even coming within sight of it only to be drawn back by the lights and action at the other end of the meadow. Some come and linger in the soothing aura near the gate, but they remember other pressing matters and retreat back to the meadow, some to return, many never to return by this path.

There are others, the Wigglesworths, the John G. Lakes, the Roland Bucks who not only live by the gate, but occasionally pass back and forth through it until one day they pass through to the Eternal never to return to this side.

The Gate to the Eternal is where Jesus desires all Christians to dwell until, they too, "pass through." One does not have to be a "special saint" to reside there, only to desire to, and act upon that desire to walk that path, to touch the gate, and experience the ambience of Heaven.[iii]

I don't know about you, but I'll take the cushioned path with beautiful wildflowers and trees and a peaceful refuge from the world and an easy "pass through" to an even more beautiful place someday. I'm tired of the "noise" of this world, aren't you? That is all the world seems able to offer these days–a lot of cacophonous noise. We have to live in a bunch of that, but there is a place of temporary refuge while here and permanent sanctuary when we pass through. We get there by "the Walk."

Some people behave as if or think that Christianity is cliquish, however, the real Christianity is anything but an exclusive group of "perfect" people. All one has to do is look at all the major Bible characters and the men that Jesus picked out as His inner circle. There are those who attempt to make Christianity an exclusive "club" meaning people have to be "acceptable" to join. This is the old "putting the cart before the horse" example which is, most certainly, not genuine Christian faith. God does not put new believers into a "Christian cookie cutter." You do not have to fit in a "mold."

All the way back in 1948, a well-known prophet, author, and preacher of the Word, A. W. Tozer said it this way:

> Pick at random a score of great saints whose lives and testimo-
> nies are widely known. Let them be Bible characters or well
> known [sic] Christians of post-Biblical times. You will be struck
> instantly with the fact that the saints were not alike. Sometimes
> the unlikenesses [sic] were so great as to be positively glaring.
> How different for example was Moses from Isaiah; how different
> was Elijah from David; how unlike each other were John and
> Paul, St. Francis and Luther, Finney and Thomas à Kempis. The
> differences are as wide as human life itself: differences of race,
> nationality, education, temperament, habit and personal qualities.
> Yet they all walked, each in his day, upon a high road of spiritual
> living far above the common way.[iv]

Having a mentor when you are learning more about the "walk" is good, but you do not have to or need to be like that person in all ways. God expects you to be yourself except for the changes that He will help you to attain. He wants you to strive to be like Jesus as a model, but you aren't going to run around in a robe and sandals speaking Aramaic and Hebrew and arguing with Pharisees either. (Well, we do have some "Pharisees" today and you might end up having to deal with them, but let's let God "argue" with them.) We are not a sect of Judaism. Christianity is the outcome of Judaism. It has fulfilled and replaced it, so please do not follow the example of some who start practicing Jewish rites and wearing Jewish religious items. The early Apostles were fighting this backpedalling trend two thousand years ago.

Religion versus Relationship

In Christian circles, we often use the jargon word my "walk" or that person's "walk" with the Lord. What does that mean? Does that mean he or she is following a set of "rules and traditions" required by the denomination they belong to? No, but that is what most people think Christianity is–following rules and traditions laid down by men to try to gain acceptance by God. This is completely backwards! The old idiom, just quoted, about "putting the cart before the horse" is not even appropriate as real Christianity does not entail pulling (or pushing!) a cart full of rules and traditions to live by at all.

There are a lot of "Christians" who consciously or unconsciously believe that following rules and traditions is the way it is supposed to be done. This is what some of us believers in Jesus (and college professors) call "religion" or "religious" practices. Following them does not a Christian make! Jesus said this about the religious experts and authorities of His time (those who practiced "religion"), "⁴They crush people with *unbearable religious demands* [my italics] and never lift a finger to ease the burden" (Matthew 23:4, NLT).

He went on to say that they did it for "show." In other words, to show everyone how righteous and holy they were. Some people still do that either to impress themselves; other people or to try to impress God. God is not impressed by men's efforts to curry His favor. In fact, the prophet Isaiah says in addressing

God, "⁶We are all like one who is unclean, all our so-called righteous acts are like a menstrual rag in your sight. We all wither like a leaf; our sins carry us away like the wind" (Isaiah 64:6, NET). Before you freak out–that is what Isaiah literally said prophetically.

Putting on "airs" of phony righteousness is absolutely revolting to God. The *New English Translation* (NET) is one of the first translations to correctly translate this verse. Historically, translators have been reluctant to put the real meaning there because it is "offensive." ("Mom, call 911, dad just fainted when he read a dirty word in this new Bible you bought him!") Well, God (through Isaiah) meant it to be offensive to tell us just how disgusting our version of righteousness is to Him! The same "disgusting" comparison is used in Isaiah 30:22 for the idols of silver and gold the Israelites were worshipping—both in the 2011 *New International Version* (NIV) and the *New English Translation* (NET)! To put it as "filthy rags" (are those oil-soaked shop rags, baby cleanup rags, or household cleaning rags?) demeans the emphasis on how horridly phony, put-on human righteousness really is to God. (Well, baby cleanup rags are kind of disgusting!) This "emphatic emphasis" should be passed on as God gave it.

This isn't the only place where translators have been reluctant to be "obscene." In the book of Romans, the Apostle Paul states, "⁸Yea doubtless and I count all things but loss for the excellency of the knowledge of Christ Jesus my Lord: for whom I have suffered the loss of all things, and do count them but dung, that I may win Christ..." (Philippians 3:8, KJV). The NIV says it this way, "⁸But even beyond that, I consider everything a loss in comparison with the superior value of knowing Christ Jesus my Lord. I have lost everything for him, but what I lost I think of as *sewer trash*, so that I might gain Christ."

In this case only the *King James Version* (KJV) and the *Common English Bible* (CEB) call this comparison what it was–dung (feces) or sewer-trash (an oblique way of saying human feces). Others normally use garbage (which isn't very offensive) or one uses trash. In fact, the full translation would be human feces. That is a pretty disgusting comparison. So, according to Paul, if a person is trying to convince people and God of their righteousness by their own efforts, that is as offensive to God as human feces is to us! Again, the emphasis was there for a purpose and should be translated correctly. The emphasis between human "righteousness" and God's is important. "Obscene" is in the use, not necessarily the word. A "normal" word can be used obscenely.

So, therefore, how do we obtain real righteousness? First, let's define it. Righteousness, according to the online "The Free Dictionary" by Farlex is being:

right·eous (rī′ chəs)
adj.
1. Morally upright; without guilt or sin: *a righteous parishioner.*
2. In accordance with virtue or morality: *a righteous judgment.*
3. Morally justifiable: *righteous anger.*

We know that God won't accept it if our righteousness is only generated by ourselves, so how do we get it right. We don't have to "prove anything" to Him for He has already made "unbearable religious burdens" unnecessary. In Matthew's account of His life, Jesus says, "[28] Come to me, all you who are struggling hard and carrying heavy loads, and I will give you rest. [29]Put on my yoke, and learn from me. I'm gentle and humble. And you will find rest for yourselves. [30]My yoke is easy to bear, and my burden is light" (Matthew 11:28-30, CEB).

This is quite unlike the ancient Pharisee or the modern legalist's version of righteousness. When we allow Jesus to put His "yoke" upon us and start pulling with Him in harness (two oxen pulled together), He gives us our righteousness through our hearts. He helps us be righteous. It is as simple as that. Paul states in his letter to the Galatians, "[16]Knowing that a man is not justified by the works of the law, but by *the faith of Jesus Christ* [my italics], even we have believed in Jesus Christ, that we might be justified by *the faith of Christ* [my italics] and not by the works of the law: for *by the works of the law shall no flesh be justified* [my italics]." Galatians 2:16 (KJV) A few modern translations, also, use "of" instead of "in" between faith and Jesus but they say "faithfulness" of Jesus Christ.

The *Common English Bible* (CEB) follows the same logic as the KJV when it states, "¹⁶However, we know that a person isn't made righteous by the works of the Law, but rather through the *faithfulness of Jesus Christ* [my italics]." We ourselves believed in Christ Jesus so that we could be made righteous by the *faithfulness of Christ* [my italics] and not by the works of the Law—because no one will be made righteous by the works of the Law (Galatians 2:16, CEB). (When Law is capitalized in the text, it means the Mosaic Law not the man-made laws of the scribes and Pharisees.)

Both translations of this verse are correct. I believe the "faith/faithfulness of Jesus" translators to be more correct than the "faith in Jesus" translators in a manner of speaking. Jesus was and is faithful to His followers and they in turn must have faith in Him to be righteous. He was faithful enough to be willing to suffer a horrible death in order to pay for their sins!

That is because Jesus doesn't practice "religion," the putting on people's shoulders of "unbearable religious burdens." He becomes our "Friend" and helps us with the burdens we already have, without the stuff "religious" people try to load us up with! When I use the word "religious" or "religion," I am referring to men and women, individually or corporately, trying to control or manipulate how they and those they influence define or interface with God. Sorry, it doesn't work that way in the Word. Many have simply not read the Word in their "mother tongue" of modern English, so they may not comprehend it in the first place. Others just believe what they have been taught that the Bible says.

Comprehension is important. Many people simply read something and, in some cases, can even recite it. That is only knowledge level learning. Memorization may be impressive, but, unfortunately, sometimes it is often only used as "ammo in a bandolier" rather than demonstrating the individual understands it, in context. Comprehension is when you really "get it!" The Holy Spirit will help us with that, but it helps even more if you are reading it in a language you grew up with. If you expect to be able to defend what you believe or to explain it intelligently to someone who wants to know more, you must get beyond the "knowledge" level. That takes prayer, study and listening to the Holy Spirit when He speaks to you.

I stated a few paragraphs back that Jesus doesn't practice religion. He didn't come to this world and accomplish what He did in order to start just another religion, either. He came to make "religion" irrelevant. What Jesus really did was to re-establish a direct relationship with God the Father for every believer who accepts it. In Paul's long letter to the Roman believers, he said:

> [9] But you aren't self-centered. Instead you are in the Spirit, if in fact God's Spirit lives in you. If anyone doesn't have the Spirit of Christ, they don't belong to him. [10] If Christ is in you, the Spirit is your life because of God's righteousness, but the body is dead because of sin. [11] If the Spirit of the one who raised Jesus from the dead lives in you, the one who raised Christ from the dead will give life to your human bodies also, through his Spirit that lives in you. [12] So then, brothers and sisters, we have an obligation, but it isn't an obligation to ourselves to live our lives on the basis of selfishness. [13] If you live on the basis of selfishness, you are going to die. But if you put to death the actions of the body with the Spirit, you will live. [14] All who are led by God's Spirit are God's sons and daughters. [15] You didn't receive a spirit of slavery to lead you back again into fear, but you received a Spirit that shows you are adopted as his children. With this Spirit, we cry, "Abba, Father." [16] The same Spirit agrees with our spirit, that we are God's children (Romans 8:9-16, CEB).

The first parts of verse 9 and 12 is referring to the fact that trying to please God by following a lot of rules and traditions is centering on ourselves and our ability to be righteous, not Him! Beware of people who misuse the second half of verse 9 by insisting that one must exhibit in church a loud emotional outburst of "tongues" or other behaviors to "prove" they have the Spirit. The Bible does not say you have to prove that publicly to anyone. Realize that Paul is talking to Christians, so what he is saying in verse 13 is that people who rely on "religion" (are calling themselves Christian, but really just faking it) to save them from "death" aren't going to make it to Heaven! Those that change to following the Spirit will live.

Religions are normally based upon fear and in the case of the "Christian religion" (legalism) that is fear of God's non-acceptance or fear of other people's opinions or approval. Let's be honest–occasionally it is just plain manipulation and control by those in authority. That is why the United States of America was founded with no state church. In other words, no "official" government dictated denomination telling everyone how to be a Christian. Religion is man's stuff. Relationship is what true and pure Christianity is really about. Religion is man's attempt to control God (and people) while relationship is God's way to reach out to man on an individual basis!

If you are a new Christian or considering accepting Jesus Christ (not a name but a title, *Christ* is Greek for Messiah/Savior), then it would be very helpful to know what this "walk" is before starting it. All walks start somewhere and this one is no exception, except that it is not at a specific place (although later you may remember the location it happened at), but at a specific point in your life.

What is "the Walk?"

To begin "the walk" a person makes the decision and prays to God for forgiveness of all sins and requests Jesus, the Son of God, to step into the leadership position of their life. When they sincerely ask for salvation, Jesus sends the Holy Spirit to be their Helper in their new life. The event can be a very spiritually exciting moment or you may feel like, "Did anything happen?" God deals with every person as an individual according to their mental makeup. Don't expect your experience to be like anyone else's. (Pay no attention to the well-meaning zealot who tells you how it must be like his or her conversion experience. It might and might not be!) Unlike many very impersonal religions, God knows and cares for us individually. He knows our needs, our quirks, our dislikes and what we can and can't handle psychologically, consciously, and subconsciously! Mind boggling isn't it?

The Christian experience is corporate (group), but individually tailored. In fact, the corporate (the church) gets its identity from the sum of the individuals within it. This is the real church. Some churches push members to meet the criteria demanded by the organization. If the "church" is demanding you walk, talk, and dress exactly like everyone else there–run! A. W. Tozer had this to say about the relationship of individual believers and the congregation:

> Has it ever occurred to you that one hundred pianos all tuned to the same fork are automatically tuned to each other? They are of one accord by being tuned, not to each other, but to another standard to which each one must individually bow. So one hundred worshippers met together, each one looking away to Christ, are in heart nearer to each other than they could possibly be were they to become "unity" conscious and turn their eyes away from God to strive for closer fellowship. *Social religion is perfected when private religion is purified* [my italics]. The body becomes stronger as its members become healthier. The whole Church of God gains when the members that compose it begin to seek a better and a higher life.[v]

Remember making copies of copies on older copy machines? Pretty quickly you had some pretty poor quality printing. The principle is the same for people trying to be "godly" by copying other saints. This is one of the ways religious groups work. If the person being copied is a really spiritual person in the true sense, they didn't get there by copying anyone else except Jesus and you won't get there by "copying" them either. I'm not saying don't take their Godly advice or refuse their mentoring. That can be valuable, but God made you unique from everyone else. Stay unique. Don't be the "cookie cutter Christian" which are often (unknown to themselves) really phonies. Appearance and rules were the spiritual downfall of the religious leaders of Jesus time, and of some today. Don't be a copy except of Jesus's ways.

In order to make that decision, you have to have "faith." What is that? Well, if someone offers you what seems to be a really good job, before you accept it you have to believe that: 1) they will pay you; 2) there will be some other benefits to having that job over what you have now; and 3) this is definitely going to be an improvement in your human condition. You have "faith" that this acceptance is a good thing. If you've been without work for a while, it may be a very good thing!

There are a number of ways that you may have arrived at this point of having faith to reach out to God by accepting Jesus as your personal Saviour. You may, as some of us have been, "at the end of your rope" physically, emotionally, and spiritually and willing to ask God take the driver's seat–desperation. (Heard the song, "Jesus, Take the Wheel!"?) You may have met someone that there is just something incredibly intangible about, but it really feels uplifting to be around them and recently you have been thinking about spiritual things, as in God (sometimes, "the walk" rubs off on other people).

You may have come to this point logically, after intensive study of Christianity. Several well-known people became Christians by trying to prove it was a hoax. C. S. Lewis (*The Lion, the Witch, and the Wardrobe*) was one such person. Or, you simply have felt the tug of God on your heart and given in to that force.

So, let's say that you are at the point of decision. The job has been offered and it looks pretty good, but how often has something that looked pretty good turned out not so? (Do I hear you thinking, "Been there, done that!") An old example of this process of decision making is holding out a 20 dollar bill to someone and saying it is theirs. Someone desperate or unthinking will simply throw out any caution and grab it. Someone thinking about needing some extra cash will think a little bit more and tentatively reach out for it expecting some trick to be played upon them at the last moment. Someone who has studied money, like a bank cashier, may reach out, take it, and examine it to see if it is counterfeit or the real thing before really accepting it when they suddenly realize the reality and the true value of it.

Likewise, faith may seem to be impetuous, cautious, or logical but it is always from God. You say, "How can that be? I made the decision!" Yes, you did, but God will give you an initial "measure of faith" to work from. Hold on for the ride, because from that point on, He will help you to increase it. As the Apostle Paul wrote to the Roman Christians, "³Because of the grace that God gave me, I can say to each one of you: don't think of yourself more highly than you ought to think. Instead, be reasonable *since God has measured out a portion of faith to each one of you* [my italics]" (Romans 12:3, CEB).

God is Reaching Out to You

In the Vatican's Sistine Chapel, one of Michelangelo's most incredible and popular paintings is called "The Creation of Adam." In it, God is reaching out with His index finger to touch Adam's index finger as Adam is still lying on the ground. The tension in the painting is that the fingers have not quite touched yet, but God is reaching out to Adam. Usually, you only see the image of the two hands. Why? Because to the Christian, this represents God's love for man in reaching out to him, even when man is only feebly reaching out to Him. God will meet anyone seeking Him "halfway", sometimes more than halfway!

Study stories from the mission's field and you will see this repeated many, many times, even when there were no missionaries ever there before one arrived! God puts His evidences throughout nature for all to see. God will meet you "halfway" and provide you with even more faith as you "walk" with Him. Around AD 55-56 Paul stated,

> [18] God's wrath is being revealed from Heaven against all the ungodly behavior and the injustice of human beings who silence the truth with injustice. [19] This is because what is known about God should be plain to them because God made it plain to them. [20] Ever since the creation of the world, God's invisible qualities—God's eternal power and divine nature—have been clearly seen, because they are understood through the things God has made. So humans are without excuse (Romans 1:18-20, CEB).

Chapter Three

THE SPIRITUAL TWINS–FAITH AND GRACE

———❧———

I n the last chapter on "The Walk," the subject of faith was introduced in the last few paragraphs. Faith and grace, its twin, are so important in the walk that this chapter is devoted to them. It has been said that with identical twins each is always aware of the other's presence even when far away. The same can be said for grace and faith unless some human factor cuts the connection. Let's look at how they are related.

What are Faith and Grace?

You have to have energy and nourishment to do a lot of walking, even spiritually. Maybe even more so in a spiritual walk. So where do you get that spiritual energy to do the walk we talked about in the last chapter? The spiritual desire or drive is called "faith" and the nourishment for the journey is called "grace." As we look at the two together, we'll discover that they are flip sides of the same coin. It is amazing how many parallels there are to real (God created) science in the spiritual. In science, we now comprehend that matter is just another form of energy. Einstein and others tried to explain this concept ($E=mc^2$) years ago, but people, in general, didn't quite get it. They are simply flip sides of the same created thing! Likewise grace and faith are intimately intertwined.

In early America, books were too expensive for many families. Early Americans didn't have the mass production printing presses of later years. If a family owned one book, it was usually the Bible. If a book was referenced for authority on something, it was usually the Bible. Interestingly, in early colonial times, it was not just the *King James Bible* in use as many believe. The *Geneva Bible*, a study Bible written by John Calvin, John Knox, and other protestant reformers self-exiled to Geneva during the reign of "Bloody Mary" the Catholic Queen of England was also in wide use, some say wider. Actually, the *King James Bible* (or Version) was only called "The Holy Bible" until sometime in the 19th century.

But whether it was "The Holy Bible" or the *Geneva Bible*, the Bible was cherished by many of the original colonists. As late (after the Colonial Era) as 1828, Noah Webster cited Biblical sources and examples throughout his definitions in his *American Dictionary of the English Language* and there weren't demonstrations in the streets, lawsuits, media assaults, or court challenges. My, my—how times have changed! People who, today, try to claim that the USA wasn't originated in the tenets of Christianity are either ignorant, prejudiced against Christianity, have an agenda, or are playing a game of semantics. For the Christian, it is just as ignorant to claim that all our Founding Fathers were "Christians" as a few were "deists" (similar to agnostic), but still believed in the tenets of Judeo-Christianity for the USA's political and educational foundation!

Faith and Grace According to Noah Webster in 1828 (from a facsimile of the real book)

> GRACE, a. [Fr. grace; It. ~razia; Sp. gra*cia;* Ir. *grasa;* from the L. *gratia,* which is formed on the Celtic; W. *rhad,* grace, a blessing, a gratuity. The primary sense of *gratus* is free, ready, quick, willing, prompt, from advancing.
> 1. Favor; good will; kindness; disposition to oblige another; as a grant made as an act of grace.

Or each, or all, may win a lady's grace. Dryden

2. Appropriately, <u>the free unmerited love and favor of God</u>, the spring and source of all the benefits men receive from him.

    And if by grace, then it is no more of works. Rom. xi.

3. Favorable influence of God; <u>divine influence or the influence of the spirit, in renewing the heart and restraining from sin.</u>

    My *grace* is sufficient for thee. 2 Cor. xii.

4. The <u>application of Christ's righteousness to the sinner</u>.

    Where sin abounded, *grace* did much more abound. Rom. v

5. A state of <u>reconciliation to God</u>. Rom. v. 2.

6. Virtuous or religious affection or disposition, as a liberal disposition, faith, meekness, humility, patience, &c . [sic] proceeding from divine influence.

7. Spiritual instruction, improvement and edification. Eph. iv. 29.

8. Apostleship, or the qualifications of an apostle. Eph. iii. 8

9. <u>Eternal life; final salvation</u>. 1 Pet. i. 13.

10. <u>Favor; mercy; pardon</u> [my underlining for emphasis 1-10].[vi]

FAITH, n. (*Noah Webster's 1828 Dictionary*) to trust; to persuade, to draw towards any thing, to conciliate; to believe, to obey. "In the Greek Lexicon of Hederic it is said, the primitive signification of the verb is to bind and draw or lead, as ~enaa signifies a rope or cable, as does ~eua~za. But this remark is a little incorrect. *The sense of the verb, from which that of rope and binding is derived, is to strain, to draw, and <u>thus to bind or make fast</u>. A rope or cable is that which makes fast.*"[my italics and underlining]

1. Belief; the assent of the mind to the truth of what is declared by another, resting on his authority and veracity, without other evidence; the judgment that what another states or testifies is the truth. I have strong *faith* or no *faith* in the testimony, of a witness, or in what a historian narrates.

2. The assent of the mind to the truth of a proposition advanced by another; belief, on probable evidence of any kind.

3. In theology, the assent of the mind or understanding to the truth of what God has revealed. <u>Simple belief of the scriptures, of the being and perfections of God, and of the existence, character and doctrines of Christ,</u> founded on the testimony of the sacred writers <u>is called *historical or speculative faith; a faith little distinguished from the belief of the existence and achievements of Alexander or of Cesar*</u> [my italics and underlining].

4. *<u>Evangelical, justifying, or saving faith</u>, is the assent of the mind to the truth of divine revelation, on the authority of God's testimony, accompanied with a cordial assent of the will or approbation of the heart; an entire confidence or trust in God's character and declarations, and in the character and doctrines of Christ, with <u>an unreserved surrender of the will to his guidance, and dependence on his merits for salvation. In other words, that firm belief of God's testimony, and of the truth of the gospel, which influences the will, and leads to an entire reliance on Christ for salvation</u>* [my italics and underlining].[vii]

"Dead religion" practices historical or speculative faith. A living, breathing, spirit-filled individual or church practices the other kind–"evangelical, justifying, or saving faith." God is not dead and neither is faith that connects with Him, not the "Oh yeah, we believe in God" type. *The real Christian doesn't "believe" in God! He or she "knows" Him personally!* We will talk about the difference between "religion and relationship" later. Suffice, at this point, to say "religion" equals speculative/historical faith and relationship equals evangelical/justifying/saving faith! Pure Christianity is not "religion."

As in Webster's definition, faith is the act that *"binds or makes* us *fast"* to God through our connection to Him. As earlier stated, if we are serious about knowing God, our faith must be the "evangelical, justifying, or saving faith" not the "historical or speculative faith" as Webster defines it. Historical faith is merely faith of the logical mind in historical facts (or what are presented as historical facts). The author of the book of Hebrews stated evangelical faith when he wrote, "Faith is the confidence that what we hope for will actually happen; it gives us assurance about things we cannot see" (Hebrews 11:1, NLT).

Evangelical faith is "heart" faith. Mark in his Gospel says it this way, "I tell you the truth, you can say to this mountain, 'May you be lifted up and thrown into the sea,' and it will happen. But you must really believe it will happen and have no doubt in your heart" (Mark 11:23, NLT). In other words, deep down in your heart, you must believe that it will happen.

Christians are generally familiar with these scriptures, but *what does having faith really mean to me and you?* God provides the initial desire and energy to get you going. After that you have the Holy Spirit to help you develop both aspects. God provides but we have to take action. ("God helps those who help themselves" is not in the Word, but He does help those who reach out to His outstretched hand!) In the chapter on "The Walk," I quoted Paul from his letter to the Roman Christians, "[3] Because of the grace that God gave me, I can say to each one of you: don't think of yourself more highly than you ought to think. Instead, be reasonable *since God has measured out a portion of faith to each one of you* [my italics]" (Romans 12:3, CEB). It doesn't say we measured it out or developed it. God gives us the initial supply and will continue to provide both as long as we continue to receive and act upon His gracious gift of faith.

Paul described it this way, "[8] For *by grace are ye saved through faith* [my italics]; and that not of yourselves: *it is the gift of God* [my italics]" (Ephesians 2:8, KJV). Now if Paul had been speaking modern English and not ancient British, he would have said this, "[8] For it is by grace you have been saved, through faith—and this is not from yourselves, it is the gift of God" (Ephesians 2:8, NIV). I wanted to present to you this verse in these two translations because most others only say "saved by His grace" or "saved by faith in God" both of which do not catch the whole context or meaning in the translation.

I've occasionally accused the KJV or NIV (I have used both) of having tediously long sentences and obscured meanings, but it is the opposite in this case. The other translations make assumptions that people intuitively comprehend the relationship between faith and grace. We don't always intuitively figure these things out. The Holy Spirit would probably tell us if we took time to ask the right question, but "busyness" keeps us from even thinking to ask Him. (Years ago, in prayer, the Spirit told me that that is the number one problem in American Christianity–busyness! People are too busy with other things [or trying of themselves to be a Christian] to pay attention to God Himself!)

"For *by grace are ye saved through faith* [my italics]; and that not of yourselves: *it is a gift of God…*[my italics]" (KJV). "For *it is by grace you have been saved, through faith* [my italics] – and this not of yourselves, *it is a gift of God…*[my italics]" (NIV). These are just two short phrases, but contain dynamite that we often overlook when reading. We cannot believe in God without "faith" but we cannot have faith without God's gift of it to us. He "graciously" gives us faith. Without God's grace, there is no faith. Without faith, we cannot draw further on God's grace for more faith or other needful things in our lives. Forgive me if I seem redundant–*faith is absolutely essential for the Christian walk and it is NOT something we can conjure up out of ourselves*. We have a "sin nature." It is impossible for us to develop real faith on our own. We can try and some of us have tried and remember what a struggle it was until we accepted God's free gracious offer.

We receive grace and faith from the same source–God's/Jesus's Enabler–the Holy Spirit. (Webster's Dictionary 1828- Holy Ghost, or Holy Spirit, the Divine Spirit; the third person in the Trinity; the sanctifier of souls.[viii]) Taking from Webster's original definitions, we see that God makes everything possible for us in our salvation walk including the ability to have faith that He will do what He promises! Grace and faith are flip sides of the same coin, and that coin is the Power of the Holy Spirit (see figure 3-1), God, being a loving God, gives us an initial dose of faith because of His grace. If we accept His call (which is ever present), He supplies us with an unlimited supply of faith and grace in our lives so we can love and help others! We are like that poor, malnourished stray dog (or cat if you prefer) that comes to our door. Our heart reaches out to

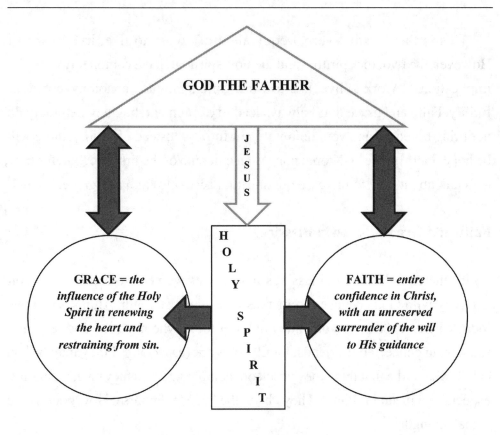

Figure 3-1 Faith and Grace

it and we provide it food and water. The animal then makes a choice–do I take this person up on their offer of food, water and love or do I remain the vagrant beggar (till animal control catches up with it) that I am. I don't know about you, but I know what my choice would be! God is offering the "food, water, and love." The devil is the dog catcher.

We have to have His grace and His faithfulness in order to function as a true believer. Paul said it this way, "To this end I labor, struggling with all *His energy* [my italics], which so powerfully works in me" (Colossians 1:29, NIV). When we take God up on His offer of grace and faith, we no longer have to struggle on our own. We now have His energy, as Paul says, to go through life's struggles. I repeat (for my sake also), *"We do not have struggle on our own!"* (Been there, done that! Don't want to do it again!)

This is the spiritual verbal equivalent of "work to live, live to work." However, the two, the spiritual and the non-spiritual, have completely opposite implications! "Work to live, live to work" infers fatigue, monotony, boredom, futility. Faith and grace don't always lead to excitement, but they definitely do not bring boredom and very definitely not futility. Instead of futility, there will be hope. Faith, grace and hope; hope is an outcome of the first two, but, for now, let's talk about how to increase our spiritual access to faith and grace.

Faith and Grace–the Twin Blessings

To increase these twin blessings in our lives we need to enhance our connectivity with God. We need to increase the signal strength. Almost everyone today carries a cell phone of some kind. For those who have one and rely on it for staying connected to friends, family, or work (especially if they may be "on call"), what is the first thing they check on their phone when they enter a building, especially a metal building? They check the "bars" of course. How good is the signal strength?

One cellular company used to do most of their advertising using the "bars" emphasizing that they had the best and most dependable coverage of all the companies. I switched to them because in many places off the beaten track, I couldn't get good reception with my former supplier. Don't you, also, want better "reception?" As Christians, we advertise that we have a connection to God—but how good is that connection? Have you checked your "bars" lately? Are you a new Christian or one who has gotten stale and want to increase your access to God? Has "busyness" cut your reception? God wants *us* to increase our reception, because He isn't the problem. He is putting out maximum power all the time. We need to move to the "location" where we get the maximum signal reception. How do we do that?

The Holy Spirit of God is the "cellular tower" through which we are enabled to communicate with God, our Creator. Jesus, the Son, "invented" this "internet." Prior to Jesus's resurrection and ascendance to Heaven, there was no internet connection to God open to all who would call on Him with their needs. In previous times, God sent angels to communicate with people (Mary, mother of Jesus; Zechariah, father of John the Baptist; Gideon; and others) and a few people had a personal relationship with God the Father–Enoch, Moses, prophets of the Old Covenant and David the King and his son Solomon for a while. But not since Adam and Eve (and there were only two of them!) had God allowed anyone desiring to come into His presence the privilege to commune with Him so intimately. In the early days of earthly kings, no one came into the king's throne room without permission from the king. In many civilizations, death or exile awaited those who disobeyed this custom! But we can come into God's throne room unannounced.

Many Christians (including myself at times) take this connection privilege for granted too lightly without appreciation for how precious this gift is. Paul, in his letter to the Romans put it this way, "Therefore, since we have been made right in God's sight by faith, we have peace with God because of what Jesus Christ our Lord has done for us. [2]Because of our faith, *Christ has brought us into this place of highest privilege where we now stand* [my italics and underline], and we confidently and joyfully look forward to sharing God's glory" (Romans 5:1, NLT).

As previously stated, as a Christian, we have a very unique personal relationship that had not existed since before Adam and Eve ate the forbidden fruit in Eden. We don't just know about God. We don't just count Him as our Saviour. We have, literally, the highest privilege of all, we have a personal relationship with God through the Holy Spirit in us, communicating through Jesus as our Mediator (could say in some instances–defense counsel) with the Father. You pray, you seek and you will experience His love which is not a theory, it is real! Once you have felt it, even for a moment, you will never doubt His existence ever again! I'm not talking "emotionalism" here. I'm talking reality!

All we have to do is put aside the busyness of modern life or our "Christian duties" and seek God first. In olden days of the American church, believers called this "praying through." Some of them had a little bit of confused theology about everything entailed with it, but that did not (in those cases) prevent the individual from receiving from God. Remember, God seeks the individual and when the individual seeks God, confused doctrine, out-of-date traditions and corrupted leaders do not stand in the way. We modern people need to set aside some times to "sharpen our blades" instead of chasing perpetually after side issues! This is what Jesus said, "[33] Seek the Kingdom of God above all else, and live righteously, and he will give you everything you need" (Matthew 6:33, NLT).

We should put some time aside to hone our relationship in longer prayer, but in order "to seek Him first," we can pray all day. What–you say! How can I do that? It is as simple as this. You think all day–right? And you probably find that at times you have some idle thought time. Aha! "Idleness is the devil's workshop" (Notinbible 13:33, NITV [Not in There Version]). But it can be depending on what we use that idle "computing" time for, so start practicing using it to talk to God. Yes, I said "talk" to God, not pray to God. People are confused and think that praying is not talking to God. Paul says, "[17] Pray without ceasing" (1 Thessalonians 5:17, KJV). When he tired of speaking King James English, he said it this way, "[17] pray continually..." (1 Thessalonians 5:17, NIV). Deciding to be more modern and colloquial, he then said, "[17] Never stop praying" (1 Thessalonians 5:17, NLT). (Actually we all know that he said it in Greek, but if he had lived for 2,000 years he might have said it all three ways.)

The point is that you can pray any time of the day or night under any circumstances good or bad as long as you have brain waves! Whether because of tradition or "just not thinking about it" many people do not seem to realize this. They think that prayer can only be in a specific position, in a specific place, under certain circumstances (usually desperation), or with a certain fervency. Not true. You can pray any time, in any place, in any circumstance! If you don't already, try it and see.

So faith, grace and prayer; they all go together tightly like a well-made jigsaw puzzle, but we don't have to figure out how to put it together ourselves like the puzzle. We ask for faith in prayer because God gave us an initial dose of faith to ask. God, through His grace, sends more faith and we begin to develop grace ourselves and a desire to pray even more. This is a good cycle to get into!

Chapter Four

TRIAL, TEMPTATION OR SIN?

Trials (Testing) and Temptation

People who say that God doesn't put people through "trials" (tests is really a better word) that can create temptations have apparently not read their Bibles in depth and context to see the truth. God, the Holy Spirit, took Jesus, also part of God but also a flesh and blood man, through a trial that most of us cannot fathom—especially we spoiled Westerners (referring to Western civilization). The theological argument as to whether He takes one through or allows one to go through 'testing' is the usual religious "clap-trap" trying to evade the simple fact that God is in control and part of that control is testing and purifying the Christian. Just as when a person is recruited as a soldier, the government doesn't just put them in a uniform and say, "You are now a soldier." It requires long-term training, sometimes extremely grueling training. If they are not physically and mentally strengthened and the proper habits of behavior developed, they will die or run away when they enter combat for the first time.

God is our Father and has every right and responsibility to shape and discipline us for our own good and for His glory. Gold and silver are purified by intense heating which causes the impurities (the dross) to rise to the top to be removed. Likewise, a diamond cutter takes an ugly stone, polishes it, looks within it to see its structure and then cuts it to its most desirable shape. Father God, who knows each of us intimately, shapes and refines us to His standards.

God even put His Son Jesus into a situation where He would be tested by Satan. And, yes, even the Messiah was tempted during this test. If you disagree, read on. It is all in scripture:

> [12] Blessed are those who endure when they are tested. When they pass the test, they will receive the crown of life that God has promised to those who love him. [13] When someone is tempted, he shouldn't say that God is tempting him. God can't be tempted by evil, and God doesn't tempt anyone. [14] Everyone is tempted by his own desires as they lure him away and trap him. [15] Then desire becomes pregnant and gives birth to sin. When sin grows up, it gives birth to death[ix] (James 1:12-15, GW).

God neither is tempted nor does He tempt anyone; however, He allows trials and testing to mold us into better Christians. Sometimes, He has to discipline us Himself. Oh, shock, feint, this author says God is "evil!" God isn't evil obviously, but you would think that people equated disciplining a wayward child as evil because they say God can ONLY allow you to go through trials to train you. He can't "spank" us Himself, they say. He can't discipline His children for that would not be Love. Not so! He is a good Father, and therefore He would be remiss if He didn't "whup our rear ends" occasionally when we ignore and disobey Him. God is Love, but discipline is part of love. Those who don't discipline (punishment is not the same thing: discipline is molding, punishment is retribution) children get negative finished results. What works as discipline for one child does not work for another. Just like a wise parent (only He is the ultimate Wise Parent) God knows each "child" intimately and knows what they require to redirect their behavior. For those of us who are a little more stubborn or dense, it is usually quite necessary for our growth:

> "My child, don't make light of the LORD's discipline, and don't give up when he corrects you. [6] For the LORD disciplines those

he loves, and he punishes each one he accepts as his child." [7]As you endure this divine discipline, remember that God is treating you as his own children. Who ever heard of a child who is never disciplined by its father? [8] If God doesn't discipline you as he does all of his children, it means that you are illegitimate and are not really his children at all. [9] Since we respected our earthly fathers who disciplined us, shouldn't we submit even more to the discipline of the Father of our spirits, and live forever? [10]For our earthly fathers disciplined us for a few years, doing the best they knew how. But God's discipline is always good for us, so that we might share in his holiness. [11]No discipline is enjoyable while it is happening—it's painful! But afterward there will be a peaceful harvest of right living for those who are trained in this way (Hebrews 12:4-11, NLT).

[17] But consider the joy of those corrected by God! Do not despise the discipline of the Almighty when you sin. [18] For though he wounds, he also bandages. He strikes, but his hands also heal… (Job 5:17-18, NLT).

This is what God said through the Prophet Samuel about King David, "[14] I will be his father, and he will be my son. If he sins, I will correct and discipline him with the rod, like any father would do" (2 Samuel 7:14, NLT).

Faith and Endurance

James, a pillar of the Jerusalem Church once said, "[2] "Dear brothers and sisters, when troubles come your way, consider it an opportunity for great joy. [3] For you know that when your faith is tested, your endurance has a chance to grow. [4] So let it grow, for when your endurance is fully developed, you will be perfect and complete, needing nothing" (James 1:2-4, NLT). He did not say that we should try to avoid having our faith tested. He did not say that you have no faith if you are being tested. He said, "Suck it up and hang in there. Rely on God. It's good for you!" Being tested is not evil nor is it a punishment from God. It is discipline to teach us endurance and to shape us for God's needs. (If you want to see punishment, read the book of Exodus and read what God did to horribly disobedient segments of the Jewish emigrants from Egypt.)

People want to ignore such scriptures as where Paul says this, "[20] But who are you, a human being, to talk back to God? "Shall what is formed say to the one who formed it, 'Why did you make me like this?'[.21] Does not the potter have the right to make out of the same lump of clay some pottery for special purposes and some for common use?" (Romans 9:20-21, NIV) If His training has formed you different from what you think it ought to be, He has a reason. The Church of Jesus Christ needs all kinds of talents and people and God shapes us to fit where He needs us to be spiritually.

Without testing (discipline) we would not develop the endurance to go on in difficult situations, the wisdom to know how, and deepen our faith in God's leadership. We would not mature or as James says, "be perfect and complete." We've all seen "spoiled" brats or adults who cannot function properly in society because they were shielded as children from the refiner's fire or diamond cutters tools. Likewise, there are some who claim the name of Jesus who have such blindly unrealistic ideas about what it means to be a Christian that they will fade at the least bit of tribulation. Jesus refers to these in His story of the sower's seeds. He said, [3] ..."Listen! A farmer went out to plant some seeds. [4] As he scattered them across his field, some seeds fell on a footpath, and the birds came and ate them. [5] Other seeds fell on shallow soil with underlying rock. The seeds sprouted quickly because the soil was shallow. [6] But the plants soon wilted under the hot sun, and since they didn't have deep roots, they died" (Matthew 13:3-6, NLT). This is only part of the parable that Jesus gave to illustrate the kinds of reasons people would forget what He taught them.

These scriptures are very relevant and you should read them all, but for this purpose, we just read through verse 6. Later, away from the crowds, Jesus's close disciples ask Him the meaning of this parable to which He replied, "[20] As for the seed that was spread on rocky ground, this refers to people who hear the word and immediately receive it joyfully. [21] Because they have no roots, they last for only a little while. *When they experience distress or abuse because of the word, they immediately fall away* [my italics]" (Matthew 13:20-21, CEB).

Endurance for the race is absolutely essential to the Christian walk as it is to any successful "walk" whether spiritual or secular. In this portion of the parable, the hearer gets excited, but never pursues a deeper relationship with God through reading the Word, prayer and communion with Jesus. They ride completely on an emotional high and drop out rather than enduring testing (the sun) to develop endurance. (The military doesn't develop Navy Seals by leading them around by the hand. They are renowned for their incredible endurance.) Without endurance we are destined to fail and to "practice" sin. Even the best believer will sin, repent, and be forgiven now and then, but "practicing sin" is not something a believer should be doing. It means the person actively indulges in sinful behavior because they have retreated from their test back to a life devoted to sin. They failed to develop "endurance."

Remember Flip Wilson (one of those entertainers we older folk knew) and his 'the devil made me do it!'? (For you younger folks, look him up on the internet or ask "grandpa.") *The devil can't make us do anything*. The devil might set you up but you are the one falling for it. As Jesus says, "[17]Anything you eat passes through the stomach and then goes into the sewer. [18] But the words you speak come from the heart — that's what defiles you. [19] For from the heart come evil thoughts, murder, adultery, all sexual immorality, theft, lying, and slander. [20] These are what defile you. Eating with unwashed hands will never defile you" (Matthew 15:16-20, NLT).

You must understand that "testing" (trials) and "tempting" are not the same thing! People get this confused all the time. If you take a test in a school or at work, the test monitor is not up there urging you to cheat. You are the one that creates that temptation (if you do have it). If you have to pass a physical test, you are the one who determines whether you will think positive, press on and succeed or have doubts which will guarantee your failure if you don't reject them immediately. In Physical Science we say that "for every action, there is a reaction." The action is neutral. The reaction can be positive or negative depending on variables. Testing is the action. Listening to temptation or rejecting temptation on your part can lead to a negative or positive reaction. Testing comes from many sources, not just God. Temptation comes from you and your reaction is strictly up to you (not the devil, not your spouse, not your friends or even your enemies–it is up to you)! If you have hung in there through various trials and tests, you will develop the endurance to succeed over temptation easily!

God must allow testing for us to become refined as a Christian. In Jesus's case, He was *led* (by the Holy Spirit) into the wilderness to face loneliness and hunger for 40 days. That's enough days to kill many people and literally start most others into the end of life downturn. Most of us would have no resistance left to temptation by the second week! But even before the testing by the devil started on Him, Jesus willingly went through a preparation that would destroy most of us!

The Testing and Temptation of Jesus Christ

The following quotation is the passage about "The Temptation of Jesus." Unfortunately, some translations state that the "Spirit led Jesus into the wilderness to be tempted." This is correct but can be easily misunderstood. Remember, God (His Holy Spirit included) does not tempt people. He tests people. He does not put temptation in their hearts. They do that. Jesus had temptations for He was as much man as He was God. The devil set up Adam and Eve with a simple lie and question. That set up a temptation in their "hearts." They were tempted to eat the forbidden fruit, but they didn't have to. Temptation is only temptation as long as it is ignored and turned down. It becomes sin when we give into it and accept its terms! Temptation itself is not sin as some people believe or even teach. If it was, none of us would have a chance! The ability to be tempted is ever present.

Jesus was put into situations where His human side could be tempted as He grew up. Elsewise, He would have been an "automaton" not a flesh and blood boy. When He entered His ministry at the age of thirty, He went through a really tough testing right away:

> The Temptation of Jesus
>
> 4 Then Jesus was led by the Spirit into the wilderness to be tempted there by the devil. ² For forty days and forty nights he fasted and became very hungry.³ During that time the devil came and said to him, "If you are the Son of God, tell these stones to become loaves of bread."⁴ But Jesus told him, "No! The Scriptures say, 'People do not live by bread alone, but by every word that comes from the mouth of God.'" ⁵ Then the devil took him to the holy city, Jerusalem, to the highest point of the Temple, ⁶ and said, "If you are the Son of God, jump off! For the Scriptures say, 'He will order his angels to protect you. And they will hold you up with their hands so you won't even hurt your foot on a stone.'"⁷ Jesus responded, "The Scriptures also say, 'You must not test the Lord your God'" (Matthew 4:1-7, NLT).

Notice what Jesus said in verse 7 or how it is translated–"You must not *test* (my italics] the Lord your God." If any temptations came to Jesus they came from his "heart" (really the soul and the flesh). Also, if they did, He didn't allow them to move over into sin. He rejected them. There are those who teach that Jesus wasn't actually tempted, but that it was the devil doing the tempting. No, the devil was doing the testing. (The devil doesn't do our thinking for us. All he can do is try to influence it.) This comes out of the notion that Jesus was purely God and since He was God could not tempt or be tempted. Jesus was not "purely" God. He was a "man-God." He was man with all the possibilities that entails and He was God. Giving up most of His privileges as part of the Godhead, He stepped down from Heaven to become a man. Paul said it this way to the Philippian Church:

⁵ You must have the same attitude that Christ Jesus had. ⁶ Though he was God, he did not think of equality with God as something to cling to. ⁷ Instead, he gave up his divine privileges; he took the humble position of a slave and *was born as a human being* [my italics]. When he appeared in human form, he humbled himself in obedience to God and died a criminal's death on a cross (Philippians 2:5-8, NLT).

He was human through and through, but He was also God! His Father was God; but He wore a human suit of flesh, which meant He could be tempted. Why? So, He could be the Messiah, the perfect mediator between sinful us and sinless God the Father. He is often referred to as our Advocate. That means defense lawyer. How could He fulfill that if He was never really tempted as some teach? Sorry folks, He was tempted in every way that a man is tempted. If that statement bothers you, that is understandable. That is why what He did so absolutely incredible. He loved us enough to give up His rights as God and be treated like and be tempted as an ordinary human. If He didn't have the capacity to be tempted, He would lack a conscience and a sense of moral responsibility and therefore be a sociopath. But He had a conscience and moral responsibility and therefore as the author of Hebrews states, "¹⁴ So then, since we have a great High Priest who has entered Heaven, Jesus the Son of God, let us hold firmly to what we believe. ¹⁵ This High Priest of ours understands our weaknesses, for he faced all of the same testings we do, yet he did not sin. ¹⁶ So let us come boldly to the throne of our gracious God. There we will receive His mercy, and we will find grace to help us when we need it most (Hebrews 4:14-16, NLT).

Most translations use the word "tempted" even one of the original English Bibles, the Geneva Bible. A few use "tested" but does it really make a difference? What sense would it make for Jesus to be tested if He was guaranteed to pass because He couldn't develop a tempting thought when enticed to do so? So, in essence, when a translation says He was tempted, it really means both. There had to be an action (test) to result in a reaction (temptation), but in all cases He rejected it and it did not become sin. And that is what is really important to us.

The Confusion (Theological) over Original Sin and Sin Nature

The confusion is over "sin nature" or "original sin." The concept of original sin has its basis in the event in the Garden of Eden when the first two humans walked and talked with God and lived an apparently very blessed life (some believe immortal). One day they disobeyed a critical command of God and lost that blessed life. They became more aware of the lusts of their bodies than their awareness of God's directions and felt shame for the first time. Here is the story:

> [21] So the Lord God caused the man to fall into a deep sleep. While the man slept, the Lord God took out one of the man's ribs and closed up the opening. [22] Then the Lord God made a woman from the rib, and He brought her to the man. [23] "At last!" the man exclaimed. "This one is bone from my bone, and flesh from my flesh! She will be called 'woman,' because she was taken from 'man.'" [24] This explains why a man leaves his father and mother and is joined to his wife, and the two are united into one. [25] Now the man and his wife were both naked, *but they felt no shame* [my italics] (Genesis 2:21, NLT).

> The Man and Woman Sin
> 3 The serpent was the shrewdest of all the wild animals the Lord God had made. One day he asked the woman, "Did God really say you must not eat the fruit from any of the trees in the garden?" [2] "Of course we may eat fruit from the trees in the garden," the woman replied. [3] "It's only the fruit from the tree in the middle

of the garden that we are not allowed to eat. God said, 'You must not eat it or even touch it; if you do, you will die.'"

[4]"You won't die!" the serpent replied to the woman. [5]"God knows that your eyes will be opened as soon as you eat it, and you will be like God, knowing both good and evil."[6]The woman was convinced. She saw that the tree was beautiful and its fruit looked delicious, and she wanted the wisdom it would give her. So she took some of the fruit and ate it. Then she gave some to her husband, who was with her, and he ate it, too. [7]*At that moment their eyes were opened, and they suddenly felt shame at their nakedness* [my italics]. So they sewed fig leaves together to cover themselves (Genesis 3:3-7, NLT).

"That" was the "original sin." When created, they lived in total harmony with God, but they failed the test Satan gave them by disobeying God's very pointed command concerning the Tree of the Knowledge of Good and Evil. They gave in to a temptation "to be like God." They lost their grace-filled existence and were now constantly tempted by the lusts they were not aware of before (verse 7). In essence, that was mankind's "Pandora's Box."

"Sin nature" is a very "slippery" term. It is not passed down through the male line which is totally scripturally unsupported, but taught as if it were a fact. It is not some mystical "whoo-whoo" aberration or aura that came upon Adam and Eve and passed on to us. There is no direct mention of a "sin nature", per se, in the Word. It is a "theological concept," but it is as simple as this: Now that Adam and Eve have "let the cat out of the bag" our bodies are ruled by the lusts of our soul and flesh unless we hold them in control. The fact that we of mankind have flesh and blood bodies without the perfect harmony that Adam and Eve (distant past) had with God at first and we shall have in our resurrected bodies (imminent future) is "sin nature." A flesh and blood body with the ability and desire to sin is sin nature. That is all it is; however, it can be another of those theological "rabbit trails" that enthrall us Christians into speculation about what this and that "really mean" and, thus, we take our eyes off of "Jesus and Him crucified." Don't let it do that to you; keep your focus on Jesus.

So the question arises, did Jesus of Nazareth have a "sin nature" or not. Theologians in the last several hundred years have argued over such "highly important" minutiae such as "how many angels can dance on the point of a needle (or head of a pin)?" The problem is that some people don't want to believe that God was "tempted", but as stated before, Jesus was both God and man. According to scriptures we have already read, He left much (how much we don't know) of His Godhood in Heaven to become a God-man. Pure God, the Trinity, was not tempted but Jesus was because He was also flesh and blood. More than enough scripture (some of which we have already read) point this out. Some people want to ignore those scriptures or "theologize" them because they are offended at the idea, but it had to be done and Jesus (God the Son) did it. You decide. It won't make any difference in your salvation whether you believe Jesus had a (quote) "sin nature" or not. He was human and was tempted and was without sin. That's good enough for me!

I like how it is summarized by Juli Camarin, the author of jcblog.net, in her article, "Jesus Was Tempted in Every Way, Yet Without Sin (Hebrews 4:15)":

> During His time on earth Jesus underwent temptation and trials so He would be fully equipped to serve as our High Priest. He dealt with difficult people and faced situations that are common in humanity and yet the Bible says that He was without sin. This is incredibly important because to defeat death we needed a perfect sin substitute. By conquering the grasp sin had on mankind He was able to free us from what held us captive. Since He emptied himself of all divine privileges and experienced the fullness of humanity, He is able to understand and empathize with us in our weaknesses. There is no one better equipped to serve before God as our High Priest than Jesus.[x]

What is Sin and Where Does It Really Come From?

The root Greek word for *sin* has something to do with an arrow missing the mark (target/bull's eye) according to various experts and that's a good description as far as it goes (no pun intended—at first). In war, to defend yourself you have to be able to shoot accurately or else you die! If you miss the mark, you are in a heap of trouble. Sin is according to Dictionary.com:

Sin-*noun, verb,* sinned, sin·ning.

noun

1. Transgression of divine law: *the sin of Adam.*
2. Any act regarded as such a transgression, especially a willful or deliberate violation of some religious or moral principle.
3. Any reprehensible or regrettable action, behavior, lapse, etc.; great fault or offense: *It's a sin to waste time.*

   verb (used without object)

4. To commit a sinful act.
5. To offend against a principle, standard, etc.[xi]

These are all true, but not the real answer. (They are the usual "beat around the bush" definitions that don't challenge the reader.) The real answer comes from reading the Word with comprehension and having a relationship with Jesus Christ. Why is there a divine law? Why were some things categorized by God as transgressions? Why are there religious or moral principles or standards? One simple reason–God loves us. Why do you tell your children, your students, your employees, your crew or your friends not to do some particular thing or group of things. Usually because they will be harmed by their actions or harm others! *"Sin" is **anything** that will hinder your Christian Walk, hurt you, damage you, or kill you (even if you aren't a Christian).* It can be sin, also, because of the effects on those closest to you–"spillover" or "collateral damage" because of your allowing temptation to become sin in your life! Anything can be a sin if used improperly or with wrong motives. **Anything**, not certain "somethings!" If it takes your focus off of God and hinders, hurts, damages, or kills you or others, it is sin! Legalism, in that context, is a sin!

For example, this does not mean if you like oysters on the half-shell that you can't eat them around someone who won't eat them, unless they live under the "law" (extra rules) and believe it is sinful. (Under the Mosaic Law, shellfish were unlawful.) If that person thinks it is a sin, it is a sin *for them*. It is a sin for you if you do it in front of them intentionally (not unintentionally).

In his letter to the Roman Christians, Paul explained it in this manner, "[20] Don't tear apart the work of God over what you eat. Remember, *all foods are acceptable* [my italics], but it is wrong to eat something if it makes another person stumble" (Romans 14:20, NLT). This doesn't mean you can't eat your raw oysters. Reading everything Paul said on this subject in Romans, the context will show that he is talking about around the offended (as he calls them "weak") Christian(s). They in turn, if they spot us in a seafood restaurant eating oysters on the half-shell are not supposed to condemn us as being "sinners" because it doesn't bother God a bit what we eat, as long as we honor Him! They will sin by condemning us unjustly; it goes beyond just food, obviously.

Why Did There Have to be a Written Law?

I am going to give an Old Testament summary to work up to the next point: God walked with Adam and Even in the Garden of Eden. They had close relationship and God was always there to advise them. After that relationship was rent asunder by their disobedience, they were evicted out of the garden to a harsher world. God still made occasional appearances to them and later to various people like Enoch (whom God liked so much He took him straight to Heaven). But people got worse and worse and finally God destroyed all people and living things (animals) but Noah, his family, and a bunch of "livestock" on a very big boat. After the flood, God began to build a new covenant relationship through Abraham and his descendants. This relationship would culminate in the birth of the Messiah predicted throughout the Old Testament. Abraham's descendants, by that time called the Israelites, ended up in Egypt with choice land and the Pharaoh's favor due to God's miraculous placement of a young Jewish man named Joseph as the Pharaoh's right-hand man during a great famine throughout the land.

However, many years later a new pharaoh took over that enslaved the Hebrew nation. God eventually rescued them and brought them out of Egypt with Moses, a Hebrew prince of Egypt (and according to secular historians a very successful Egyptian army general who conquered the Ethiopians). Historically, peoples who have been enslaved all their lives (including people who have lived in totalitarian states where your life is regulated severely) have a very difficult time adjusting to freedom and need help adjusting. Moses was leading at least 1.5 million people who had not been in charge of their own lives for possibly 2 to 3 centuries. God's plan was not at that point (Jesus life, death, and resurrection) where He could work with these people individually. Therefore, the Law was given, a written (or inscribed) code of behavior to keep Israel as a nation following God and receiving the benefits He promised them if they would obey the Law. (He did! When they obeyed the Law as a nation, He "blessed their socks off!")

Sin was codified because they did not have the Holy Spirit inside them to guide them. It no longer is codified for us as we talk about in the chapter on "The Walk." Example–personal computers no longer have to be tied into a main frame; they have everything they need to operate inside them now. We have the Holy Spirit inside of us to give us direction if we have accepted Jesus as our Saviour. We don't need "hardwiring."

How Can a Thought be a Sin?

Trial, temptation and then sin or no sin? That is the progression. The final product, sin, is our personal choice when something appeals to our flesh and our mind that would be destructive to us. Being tempted (tested and temptation arising) is not sinning unless you intentionally allow it to linger in your mind.

(No, for you "bean counters" there is no set time limit, but your conscience and the Holy Spirit will let you know!) Jesus said that committing sex with another in our minds is the same as the real thing. Jesus stated it this way, "[27]You have heard the commandment that says, 'You must not commit adultery.' [28] But I say, anyone who even looks at a woman with lust has already committed adultery with her in his heart" (Matthew 5:27-28, NLT). In other words, the guy (or gal) didn't shut it down quickly and dwelled upon the possibilities.

But you say, "If there is no physical act, there is no real sin." Oh? What is the difference between premeditated murder and manslaughter? There are varying types of manslaughter in different jurisdictions; however, in general if someone kills someone else and it is deemed manslaughter, that means the person had no intention (no plan to) not any premeditation to kill that person. It is an "accident" that happens during another event; *but murder is something that is thought out in the mind first and then acted upon.* This is what Jesus is talking about. If you dwell on the action in your mind whether it is sex, theft, or physically attacking someone, you are working out the details as if, if the opportunity presented itself, you would act upon it. Whether you actually act upon it is not important in this context. You have seriously thought about committing a physical sin, therefore it is mental sin but a sin none-the-less.

I mentioned the old 70s comedian Flip Wilson and his famous quotation "The devil made me do it!" I don't know if that was his motivation, but much humor comes out of pain, out of real life. We all want to blame the devil for our bad intentions or actions, but sin doesn't come from the devil. He may set us up for temptation, but we are the suckers that fall for it! Where does Jesus say sin comes from? He said, "[20] ...It is what comes from inside that defiles you. [21] For from within, out of a person's heart, come evil thoughts, sexual immorality, theft, murder, [22] adultery, greed, wickedness, deceit, lustful desires, envy, slander, pride, and foolishness. [23] All these vile things come from within; they are what defile you" (Mark 7:20-23, NLT).

This is the very definition of the inborn flesh and blood "sin nature" that I talked about earlier. It is part of our "makeup." It is why we need a Savior, an Advocate, a Guide which we have in Jesus and God's Holy Spirit. I like the way the God's Word translation says it (as quoted earlier), [14] Everyone is tempted by his own desires as they lure him away and trap him. [15] Then desire becomes pregnant and gives birth to sin. When sin grows up, it gives birth to death" (James 1:12-15, GW). Jesus, as we've read, was tempted in all things mankind is tempted in, yet He did not let His flesh and soul's desires become pregnant and give birth to sin. He was qualified to gain our forgiveness for our sins from God the Father.

God's Forgiveness = Jesus's Love

This is why it is so important to focus on our Saviour, Jesus, and the love coming down to us from God. Many translations in the letter called "1 Peter" say that "love covers a multitude of sins." *Cover* is what I call an indirect or conceptual word. It implies things to us. If your friend says, "I've got you covered" that could mean financially, physically against harm, many things. In general, though, we know it means the problem is taken care of. Here is how the Common English Bible says it. It is a little more specific than just saying "covers it." Peter says, "[7] The end of everything has come. Therefore, be self-controlled and clearheaded so you can pray. [8] Above all, show sincere love to each other, because *love brings about the forgiveness of many sins*[my italics] (1 Peter 4:7-8, CEB). "Brings about the forgiveness of many sins" is a much more accurate way of saying it.

Each "Gospel" (story of Jesus life by an apostle or disciple) has a different purpose, appeals to a different audience, and gives a complementary view of events so that we get the whole picture. This is why a "parallel Bible" is a handy addition to the library of a student of the Word which we all should be. The book of John and later his letters 1-3 John are all about the love of God which is what we just said covers our sins. I want to end this chapter with some verses written by John the Apostle:

[16] For God loved the world so much that he gave his one and only Son, so that everyone who believes in him will not perish but have eternal life (John 3:16, NLT).

[14] So the Word became human and made his home among us. He was full of unfailing love and faithfulness. And we have seen his glory, the glory of the Father's one and only Son (John 1:14, NLT). [16] From his abundance we have all received one gracious blessing after another. [17] For the law was given through Moses, but God's unfailing love and faithfulness came through Jesus Christ. [18] No one has ever seen God. But the unique One, who is himself God, is near to the Father's heart. He has revealed God to us (John 1:16-18, NLT).

[9] I have loved you even as the Father has loved me. Remain in my love (John 15:9, NLT).

[16] We know how much God loves us, and we have put our trust in his love. God is love, and all who live in love live in God, and God lives in them (1 John 4:16, NLT).

At the right time in our history, Jesus brought God's Love into a fallen world and spread it around to all who would love Him as their Savior. That's us! We are not condemned anymore! Not if we return His Love. We are loved by the God of Creation. That is way beyond cool!

Chapter Five

"Jesus and Him Crucified" (1Cor. 2:2)
The Source of Your Salvation

꿈

Blood, the First Sacrifice, First of Harvest, and Clean and Unclean Animals

The balance point of Christianity is Jesus death, burial and resurrection–
specifically centered on His crucifixion. It is a very horrible way to die[1];
therefore, some critics of Christianity refer to Christianity as a "bloody" religion.
Well, truth be known, it is based upon "blood." In the book of Genesis, when
the Flood was over and Noah and his family were on solid ground again, the
author of Genesis related, "9 God blessed Noah and his sons and said to them,
"Be fertile, multiply, and fill the earth. ²All of the animals on the earth will
fear you and dread you—all the birds in the skies, everything crawling on the
ground and all of the sea's fish. They are in your power. ³Everything that lives
and moves will be your food. Just as I gave you the green grasses, I now give
you everything. ⁴However, you must not eat meat *with its life, its blood, in it*
[my italics]" (Genesis 9:1-4, CEB).

The King James Version says it this way, "³Every moving thing that liveth
shall be meat for you; even as the green herb have I given you all things. ⁴But

---

1   Crucifixion for execution or extreme punishment is still occasionally used in the Middle
East and a few other places in the world. It was outlawed by Constantine I, Christian Emperor
of Rome, in AD 337 in the Roman Empire. Some Muslim countries such as Iran and Saudi
Arabia still have it "on their books" as a means of execution but "experts" say that it is seldom,
if ever, used.

flesh with the life thereof, which is the blood thereof, shall ye not eat" (Genesis 9:3-4, KJV).

The gist of this, in all translations, is that God considered the life to be in the blood. To eat blood or any animal that hadn't been "bled out" was a sin under the Old Covenant with man. But blood, also, had to be shed for transgressions of the law–sin. Some students of the Bible believe that this was instituted with God's killing of animals to make clothing for Adam and Eve from the skins. This involved the shedding of blood of the animals and the covering of the now sinful couple, who had already tried fig leaf attire to cover their newly discovered shame.

In Genesis, Moses relates, "[20] Then the man—Adam—named his wife Eve, because she would be the mother of all who live. [21] And the Lord God made clothing from animal skins for Adam and his wife" (Genesis 3:20-21, NLT). This was before He evicted them from the Garden so they wouldn't have access to immortality (The Tree of Life) as they had already helped themselves to the other forbidden Tree of the Knowledge of Good and Evil. Whether the "buckskins" were for their modesty or protection from the elements when evicted from the Garden, God doesn't say. It is not a doctrinal issue (except to a very few), but it does fit into the pattern of a "sacrifice."

The First Recorded Sacrifice (Recorded as a Sacrifice)

Much later, the Mosaic Law set forth specific requirements for sacrifices, but sometime after being evicted from the Garden, Adam's family had already begun making sacrifices to God. In Genesis chapter 4 we see this event transpire:

> [3] When it was time for the harvest, Cain presented some of his crops as a gift to the Lord. [4] Abel also brought a gift—the best of the firstborn lambs from his flock. The Lord accepted Abel and his gift, [5] but he did not accept Cain and his gift. This made Cain very angry, and he looked dejected.

⁶"Why are you so angry?" the Lord asked Cain. "Why do you look so dejected? ⁷You will be accepted if you do what is right. But if you refuse to do what is right, then watch out! Sin is crouching at the door, eager to control you. But you must subdue it and be its master." ⁸One day Cain suggested to his brother, "Let's go out into the fields." And while they were in the field, Cain attacked his brother, Abel, and killed him (Genesis 4:3-8, NLT).

There are no specifics this early in Genesis about how they were supposed to do their sacrifices, but since God still spoke to Adam and his family perhaps there were requirements that they understood. Later, under the Mosaic Law, the sacrificial animal or produce had to be perfect, not blemished in any way. It had to be the best among the first you had from the flock or harvest. A positive attitude of giving was important also. Perhaps, Cain² offered blemished, second-rate, later gathered stuff, but he had the choice, from God, of doing it again properly and it would be accepted. But he chose to get mad at God instead and to kill his brother out of jealousy. Cain probably had an attitude issue to begin with.

There were sacrifices that early to at least show submission to God's authority and perhaps to pay for their sins. It doesn't specifically say other than it was given as a gift to God. It may have been the same form of sacrifice that God codified centuries later in the Mosaic Law. We do know that in some point in the pre-Flood world, that they understood the concept of "clean" animals and "unclean" animals which was also codified in the Law later. In Noah's preparation for his "voyage" these were some of his instructions, "7When everything was

---

2   Cain goes on to marry in another village. The anti-Christian argument is "How could he marry someone if Adam and Eve were the only parents and it was just him, Abel (now dead) and Seth?" In the old movie about the Scopes Monkey Trial this question ends the defense of Biblical history and Creationism. It shouldn't have. In Genesis chapter 5, it says that after Seth's birth, Adam lived another 800 years and had "other sons and daughters." Reasonable to assume he had other sons and daughters besides Cain and Abel before Seth came along. Adam lived 930 years and was apparently fertile most of that time. There were 8 generations producing children in Adam's lifetime and their children producing children. And, yes, by standards set centuries later this would be incest, but was apparently not a stigma or genetic problem in that era. Life spans gradually decreased to 120 years by Jacob's generation 14 generations after Noah.

ready, the Lord said to Noah, "Go into the boat with all your family, for among all the people of the earth, I can see that you alone are righteous. [2] Take with you seven pairs—male and female—of each animal I have approved for eating and for sacrifice, and take one pair of each of the others. [3] Also take seven pairs of every kind of bird. There must be a male and a female in each pair to ensure that all life will survive on the earth after the flood" (Genesis 7:1-3, NLT).

The NLT Bible is one of only a few translations that say "…seven pairs—male and female- of each animal I have approved for eating and sacrifice…" Most other versions only say "of clean" animals. God-followers of that era, Moses and his family apparently knew what "clean" and "unclean" animals were. Later codified in the Mosaic Law, only clean animals could be eaten or sacrificed. Was the NLT stretching it by deriving "eating and sacrifice" out of "clean?" Not hardly, since right after Noah was able to leave the ship on to dry land again, he offered sacrifices out of his stock of clean animals, "[20] Then Noah built an altar to the Lord, and there he sacrificed as burnt offerings the animals and birds that had been approved for that purpose" (Genesis 8:20, NLT).

An interesting "side-note" is that they carried clean and unclean animals on the ark, sacrificed clean animals on the altar, but God told Noah, "[3] *Everything that lives and moves* [my italics] will be your food. Just as I gave you the green grasses, I now give you everything. [4] However, you must not eat meat with its life, its blood, in it" (Genesis 9:3-4, CEB). Thousands of years before, God had blessed Adam and Eve and said to them, "Be fertile and multiply; fill the earth and master it. Take charge of the fish of the sea, the birds of the sky, and everything crawling on the ground." [29] Then God said, "I now give to you all the plants on the earth that yield seeds and all the trees whose fruit produces its seeds within it. These will be your food" (Genesis 1:28-29, CEB).

It appears that we were originally vegetarians (at least those who obeyed God), which I am sure some healthy vegetarians are going to beat us meat eaters over the head with, but God gave us meat to eat after the flood. So who is right? No one is wrong. In a subsequent chapter, we will examine how God told us through the Apostle Paul, that for the New Covenant believer there would be no "clean" and "unclean" foods, meat or otherwise. Whatever people felt right about eating, or not eating, would be up to them, as long as they gave thanks to God for it! (See Romans 14.)

It would appear that, since Noah and his family were on real estate that had to regenerate plant life and animals multiply and not to use up the few clean animals they had for breeding stock, God did not establish the clean requirement for their diet at that time. Meat had been added to their diet after the flood according to the wording; but, also, this is the point where God says (now that you can eat meat) you must not consume the blood. Later, the Mosaic Law would codify the "clean" animals for eating requirement after the Israelites (in Moses time) had developed from a small family group to well over one million people. It also codified sacrifice.

Codification of Sacrifices to God

Making sacrifices to God of clean animals had been established in the pre-Flood world and carried over, by God's command, into the new world that Noah and his family would establish. Approximately 14 centuries later, Moses is leading the freed slave nation of Israel out of Egypt when God gives him the Law by which the Israelites are commanded to live. This we refer to as the Mosaic Law; although, in the New Testament it is mentioned as the Law of Moses, Mosaic Law, Law, Jewish law or just "law." In some translations, you must figure out by context whether the author is referring to the "law" consisting of the Law of Moses burdened down with the laws added by the scribes and Pharisees, or simply the Mosaic Law or as the new "law" that the Apostle Paul calls the law of Christ, "[21] When I am with the Gentiles who do not follow the Jewish law, I too live apart from that law so I can bring them to Christ. But I do not ignore the law of God; I obey the law of Christ" (1 Corinthians 9:21, NLT).

In giving the Law to Moses, God reconfirms the tenets of sacrifice we have already seen except for an addition. God tells Moses, "[29] Don't delay offering the produce of your vineyards and winepresses. Give me your oldest son. [30]

Do the same with your oxen and with your sheep. They should stay with their mother for seven days. On the eighth day, you should give them to me" (Exodus 22:29-30, CEB). God required the "sacrifice" of the first son of a family; however, it was symbolic sacrifice. Previous to these commands, God had made another, [2] "Consecrate to me every firstborn male. The first offspring of every womb among the Israelites belongs to me, whether human or animal"(Exodus 13:2, NIV). So, was that "consecration" to be short-lived? No, for God later tells Moses, [19] "Every first male offspring is mine, even the firstborn males of all your livestock, whether cattle, sheep, or goats. [20] It will cost you a sheep or a goat to buy back the firstborn donkey. If you don't buy it back, then you must break the donkey's neck. *You must buy back every firstborn of your sons* [my italics]. No one may come into my presence without an offering" (Exodus 34:19-20, GW).

Under the Law of Moses, the first-born son of every Jewish family belonged to God. It did not mean he became a priest unless he was in the priestly line from Aaron. However, this gave him special privileges in inheritance and responsibilities in the family. Being the first- born was very important in Old Testament times. "First-born" or "first-harvest" would later take on a whole new dimension in the New Covenant.

The idea of the "sacrifice" of the first-born son was familiar to any Jew who was familiar with their genealogical history. As a test of his dedication and faith, God had ordered Abraham, the father of nation of Israel, to sacrifice his son (precursor to what God actually did a long time later with His Son), but stopped him at the last minute and provided a ram for the sacrifice. Since Abraham, reluctantly but obediently, did what God asked (Jehovah God never asked for human sacrifice!) then God considered him a righteous man and made the promise we mentioned–the Messiah would come as one of Abraham's descendants! This was the beginning of the nation of Israel (see Genesis 22). The ram for Isaac was the first substitutionary sacrifice approximately 5 centuries prior to the Law codifying this practice. All of it pre-dates what God had in His plan, when in the "fullness of time" He would bring relationship back to

His children who accepted His offer by sacrificing His own Son through the Crucifixion for the sins of humanity.

Jesus Christ–the Ultimate and Final Sacrifice for Sin

The author of Hebrews explains how Jesus became the ultimate Sacrifice that replaced the Old Covenant method:

Christ Is the Perfect Sacrifice

> [11] So Christ has now become the High Priest over all the good things that have come. He has entered that greater, more perfect Tabernacle in Heaven, which was not made by human hands and is not part of this created world. [12] With his own blood—not the blood of goats and calves—he entered the Most Holy Place once for all time and secured our redemption forever. [13] Under the old system, the blood of goats and bulls and the ashes of a young cow could cleanse people's bodies from ceremonial impurity. [14] Just think how much more the blood of Christ will purify our consciences from sinful deeds so that we can worship the living God. For by the power of the eternal Spirit, Christ offered himself to God as a perfect sacrifice for our sins. [15] That is why he is the one who mediates a new covenant between God and people, so that all who are called can receive the eternal inheritance God has promised them. For Christ died to set them free from the penalty of the sins they had committed under that first covenant (Hebrews 9:11-15, NLT).

The book of Hebrews goes on to say:

> 10 The old system under the law of Moses was only a shadow, a dim preview of the good things to come, not the good things

themselves. The sacrifices under that system were repeated again and again, year after year, but they were never able to provide perfect cleansing for those who came to worship. [2] If they could have provided perfect cleansing, the sacrifices would have stopped, for the worshipers would have been purified once for all time, and their feelings of guilt would have disappeared.[3] But instead, those sacrifices actually reminded them of their sins year after year. [4] For it is not possible for the blood of bulls and goats to take away sins. [5] That is why, when Christ came into the world, he said to God, "You did not want animal sacrifices or sin offerings. But you have given me a body to offer.[6] You were not pleased with burnt offerings or other offerings for sin.[7] Then I said, Look, I have come to do your will, O God—as is written about me in the Scriptures.'" [8] First, Christ said, "You did not want animal sacrifices or sin offerings or burnt offerings or other offerings for sin, nor were you pleased with them" (though they are required by the law of Moses). [9] Then he said, "Look, I have come to do your will." *He cancels the first covenant in order to put the second into effect* [my italics]. [10] For God's will was for us to be made holy by the sacrifice of the body of Jesus Christ, once for all time.[11] Under the old covenant, the priest stands and ministers before the altar day after day, offering the same sacrifices again and again, which can never take away sins. [12] But our High Priest offered himself to God as a single sacrifice for sins, good for all time. Then he sat down in the place of honor at God's right hand. [13] There he waits until his enemies are humbled and made a footstool under his feet. [14] For by that one offering he forever made perfect those who are being made holy (Hebrews 10:1-14, NLT).

So now we don't need animal sacrifices or, for that matter, written laws to be walk in peace with our Creator. Jesus was the culmination of the Old Covenant and began the New. Now that He has paid the final price for mankind's sin, we have direct access to God through Him. We accept Him for our Saviour and we have salvation. At that point, we are "saved." It requires nothing else to become saved, but we do have to walk it out every day.

What Does Walking Out Your Salvation or Being Saved Mean?

"Not by might nor by power, but by my Spirit," says the LORD Almighty (Zechariah 4:6, NIV). You may have heard this quoted from time to time (or maybe not). The full quote from the book of Zechariah the prophet says, "⁶Then he said to me, "This is what the Lord says to Zerubbabel: It is not by force nor by strength, but by my Spirit, says the Lord of Heaven's Armies. ⁷Nothing, not even a mighty mountain, will stand in Zerubbabel's way; it will become a level plain before him! And when Zerubbabel sets the final stone of the Temple in place, the people will shout: 'May God bless it! May God bless it!'"(Zechariah 4:6-7, NLT) [3] The "he" in this scripture is God Almighty speaking to Zechariah about relying on His [the power of] Spirit rather than their human power as they took on the task of rebuilding not only the Temple, but the Jewish nation. This sums up how we must also approach our walk in salvation. The "final stone" will be when we go to be with the Lord and if we are walking with Him, He will level some pesky "mountains" during our walk.

Previously, we've discussed the role of the Holy Spirit in the life of the believer in helping them to walk the "Walk." We have talked some about how there are those who want to retreat to living under "law" rather than grace and to inflict that regression onto other Christians. As Paul told the Philippian Church, "²Watch out for those dogs, those people who do evil, those mutilators who say

---

3   King Cyrus of Medes and Persians, after conquering the Babylonians, began to set the Israelite captives free to go home and to begin to rebuild the Jewish Temple. (Isaiah the prophet prophecied that a king named Cyrus would conquer the formidable Babylonians and free the Jews to go home. This was 80 years before the Israelites were even conquered and taken to Babylon, 120 years before Cyrus' conquest, and 130 years before he freed the Jews!) Years later, King Darius reaffirmed Cyrus decree and appointed Zerubbabel as governor over the province of Judah and, once again, gave him permission to rebuild the Jewish temple.

you must be circumcised to be saved. [3] For we who worship by the Spirit of God are the ones who are truly circumcised. We rely on what Christ Jesus has done for us. We put no confidence in human effort..." (Philippians 3:2-3, NLT) There are always two groups of distractors that the believer must deal with as the Christians of Paul's time did. These are: 1) those who want to play with or go back under the Law and take others with them (Judaizers) or create a new system of laws (legalists) and 2) those who misuse the idea of doing away with "works" and proclaim a "lazy" version of grace.

First Distractor–Judaizing or "Toe the Line-We are still under the Law"

It bothers me when I see or hear a Christian (especially non-Jewish) who has become absolutely captivated by (not just studying) Jewish traditions, the Law, Jewish festivals, rituals, *ad infinitim* and begin to teach them to other Christians as if they are essential to their Christian walk. (It is interesting and enlightening, especially since many traditions are prophetic of the Messiah, but not essential.) On television, I see non-Jewish Christians putting on Jewish religious garments and promoting Jewish ways of thinking. Paul was dealing with this regressive issue already in his time and Paul was a "Jew's Jew" (But "now" he was a follower of the Messiah).

People feel safer when they can build or borrow fortifications of traditions, rules and laws to place between themselves and the world. Personally, I believe many do it to build a wall between themselves and God; they are "scared to death" of a personal relationship with God through Jesus Christ. They want to feel "safe" through a religious façade, unwilling to go any further into the Holy of Holies that God has opened now for believers. The curtain was torn in two as we just read both literally during Jesus's death and eternally in the spiritual sense. Sometimes, people think they have to be "special" to get closer to God; they don't. That is why in the Bible, Old and New Testaments, God the Father and God the Son, Jesus, picked ordinary people and sometimes scoundrels and undesirables (a Jewish IRS agent) to become His workers. You don't have to be special. You are "special" after being saved.

Trying to build a wall of legalism or returning to the Law will cause a person to cut themselves off from God, not vice versa. This is what Paul said about this issue, "[10] For all who rely on the works of the law are under a curse, as it is written: *Cursed is everyone who does not continue to do underline everything written in the Book of the Law* [my italics & underline]." [11] Clearly no one who relies on the law is justified before God, because "the righteous will live by faith." [12] The law is not based on faith; on the contrary, it says, "The person who does these things will live by them" (Galatians 3:10-12, NIV).

Christians are the "righteous" in verse eleven and we live by faith, not the Law and its strictures. He goes on to tell the Galatian believers when they were being urged by the Judaizers of their day to be circumcised (and obey the Law of Moses), "[2] Listen! I, Paul, tell you this: If you are counting on circumcision to make you right with God, then Christ will be of no benefit to you. [3] I'll say it again. If you are trying to find favor with God by being circumcised, you must obey every regulation in the whole law of Moses. [4] *For if you are trying to make yourselves right with God by keeping the law, you have been cut off from Christ! You have fallen away from God's grace* [my italics] (Galatians 5:2-4, NLT). That is pretty strong! Doesn't sound to me like Paul is saying we are still under the Law.

There are those who say that we are not subject only to the extra laws the scribes and Pharisee made up, but Paul says, "…the whole law of Moses…." Circumcision was part of the Law of Moses not an added Pharisaical law. Be very careful about thinking you *must* follow parts of the Law. Some of those who say we are still "under the law" split hairs and say that the circumcision issue is separate. It was one part of the Law like a rudder is one part of a ship. There are many parts to the Law and many parts of a ship. If the ship is still "ship-worthy" you can't just take part of it home with you (I'm not talking about towels off a cruise ship). You've got to take it all. (Better have a really big SUV and trailer!) If you dabble with the Law because you think or are taught you have to–guess what? You have to take it all and you leave faith and grace behind!

Paul consistently, especially in the Romans letter, praises the Law of Moses as being good. However, he points out repeatedly that we are NO LONGER OBLIGATED TO FOLLOW THE LAW! (See Galatians letter.) I've read articles in which the authors say we are still under the law and the Holy Spirit now helps us follow it. That is absurd! How much of it? What parts of it? Paul repeatedly says that if we do, we give up grace and have to follow the whole Law! The Holy Spirit, Jesus's sacrifice and our connection to God through them replaced the need for a law. Here's what Paul had to say about that:

> [18] For if *the inheritance* [my italics] could be received by keeping the law, then it would not be the result of accepting God's promise. But God graciously gave it to Abraham as a promise. [19] Why, then, was the law given? *It was given alongside the promise* [my italics] to show people their sins. *But the law was designed to last only until the coming of the child who was promised* [my italics]. God gave his law through angels to Moses, who was the mediator between God and the people. [20] Now a mediator is helpful if more than one party must reach an agreement. But God, who is one, did not use a mediator when he gave his promise to Abraham. [21] Is there a conflict, then, between God's law and God's promises? Absolutely not! *If the law could give us new life, we could be made right with God by obeying it.* [22] *But the Scriptures declare that we are all prisoners of sin, so we receive God's promise of freedom only by believing in Jesus Christ* [my italics].

God's Children through Faith

> [23] Before the way of faith in Christ was available to us, we were placed under guard by the law. We were kept in protective

custody, so to speak, until the way of faith was revealed. [24] Let me put it another way. *The law was our guardian until Christ came; it protected us until we could be made right with God through faith.* [25] *And now that the way of faith has come, we no longer need the law as our guardian* [my italics]. [26] For you are all children of God through faith in Christ Jesus (Galatians 3:18-26, NLT).

The "inheritance" in the first verse is the promised relationship we now have through the Messiah—Jesus. Notice that he said the Law was "alongside" the Promise, not part of the Promise (verse 19). Trying to live by the Law of Moses or part of it is not part of the Salvation process for a Christian.) Notice, again, that he is referring to the law given by God to Moses not the Pharisaical laws added later. To the contrary, it will hinder us as Paul says repeatedly. He says many other things to reinforce this in the Galatian letter:

[12] Dear brothers and sisters, I plead with you to live as I do in freedom from these things, for I have become like you Gentiles— free from those laws (Galatians 4:12, NLT).
[17] The Spirit and your desires are enemies of each other. They are always fighting each other and keeping you from doing what you feel you should. [18] *But if you obey the Spirit, the Law of Moses has no control over you* [my italics] (Galatians 5:17-18, CEV).
[13] *Christ redeemed us from the curse of the law* [my italics] by becoming a curse for us, for it is written: "Cursed is everyone who is hung on a pole" (Galatians 3:11, NIV).

To gain and grow our salvation through still adhering to the Law of Moses would be utter legalism. We wouldn't have time for our relationship to God because of all the rules we would have to be sure to follow. Followers of the Law did not and do not now have a personal relationship with Jesus the Christ. We do! *Our salvation is by faith, not following rules!* The essence of God's intent of those "rules" is "written on our hearts" not on clay, paper, or in an electronic device. We live them out spiritually if we follow the Holy Spirit's guidance. To say and/or try to incorporate the Law into our walk of salvation is like going back to the high school or college we graduated from, spitting on our diploma as we are giving it back to the school and going back to the freshman class. *We (our spiritual ancestors) have been there and we do not go back there! We are in the "graduated" class.*

Legalism is a ball and chain, not a liberator. Legalism can be "Judaizing" by going back to the Law of Moses again or it can be trying to establish a "law" of the New Testament much as the scribes and Pharisees established multitudes of "laws" redefining the simpler ones of Moses. Either way, it is very, very wrong! It puts the disciple's eyes on paper and ink being his or her salvation instead of the Saviour–Jesus. *Complexity leads to legalism. Simplicity leads to Christ.* In Paul's first letter to the Corinthian Church he expresses it this way, "2 And so it was with me, brothers and sisters. When I came to you, I did not come with eloquence or human wisdom as I proclaimed to you the testimony about God. [2] For I resolved to know nothing while I was with you except Jesus Christ and him crucified. [3] I came to you in weakness with great fear and trembling. [4] My message and my preaching were not with wise and persuasive words, but with a demonstration of the Spirit's power, [5] so that your faith might not rest on human wisdom, but on God's power" (1 Corinthians 2:1-5, NIV). Paul strived in his teaching to keep it simple.

Salvation and being "saved" are different and yet the same; salvation is an ongoing process in the life of the believer. Being "saved" can refer to the act of accepting Jesus as our Master and Savior or it can refer to the spiritual condition of the believer. It is more of an adjective, a descriptive of the spiritual condition of the saint; whereas, "salvation" is a noun, a fact, a process of deepening our relationship with God. Salvation is a way of life, every day of our lives. A. W. Tozer summed up salvation this way, "Essentially salvation is the restoration of a right relation between man and his Creator, a bringing back to normal of the Creator-creature relation."[xii] (The restoration of what Adam and Eve lost for mankind.) This restoration is ongoing and it is accomplished through faith and the grace of our Lord, Christ Jesus, not by following rules. Walking in "faith and grace" and following legal requirements are not even in the same galaxy!

Second Distractor – Lazy or "Relevant" Christianity

We are in the image of God; therefore, we have a need to create things. We like to "make things happen." And, occasionally, we make someone mad at us for "making something happen" when all they really wanted was for us to listen to what they had to say. Sound familiar to you married guys? I'll use that example because guys are hardwired to "fix things" and when a wife (who likes to share and talk things out) brings up something that isn't working right, we immediately have to fix it, or as the saying goes–"die trying." One hour ago, my wife told me of her problems with her new cellphone which is doing some really weird stuff. She didn't want me to fix it. She knows that although I'm a do-it-yourselfer in most things, electronics are way out of my league. She just wants to share it with me. But you know what? Typical male reaction–I'm sitting there at my computer writing this chapter and thinking how guilty I feel for not being able to fix it. We are just that way. We men are worse, but both sexes want to fix things on their own when they really should be listening because Someone (notice it is capitalized) just wants to relate to them.

The Law of Moses was "works." As Paul tries to explain in the book of Romans when referring back to God's relationship with Abraham, God made Abraham a promise (see Romans chapter 4). That promise was essentially that his "seed" (He did not say seeds as Paul points out) would someday bless the world. That was the promise of the coming Messiah. Again, as Paul points out the Law of Moses and the Promise are not the same thing. They both applied to the Jews, but were very different avenues toward the same "destination." The Promise was fulfilled when Jesus of Nazareth paid the price for mankind's sins by undergoing crucifixion and then being resurrected to a glorified body and becoming our

Savior. The Law was given to keep a bunch of unruly, disobedient former slaves (about a million and one-half experts say) behaving at least marginally well. If you think that all those people in the Old Testament were the very vision of a "saint" you need to read the Old Testament. It is one of the greatest "soaps" ever written (because it is about real people)!

The Law, as we saw in the first distractor section, was a schoolmaster, a tutor, a guardian to keep the Jewish nation moving in the right direction toward that "fullness of time" when Jesus, the Messiah, would come and fulfill all the over 300 prophecies and references to the coming of the Messiah. When He came, as Paul said, the Law ceased to be our guide and the Holy Spirit and Jesus *replaced it*. (Again, refer to scriptures in previous section.) We left "works" behind and stepped into "grace and faith." (At the risk of being redundant–"Not even in the same galaxy!") Suffice to say, we listen to God now. *We don't have to "fix" anything!* It's been permanently fixed for eternity! *Leave "it" alone. Walk with God, not a list of requirements.*

This section of the chapter started with the quotation from the book of Zechariah from the Old Testament. In it Zechariah says that God said, "Not by might nor by power, but by my Spirit," says the LORD Almighty (Zechariah 4:6, NIV). In those days, the Spirit of God worked outside of His followers. In our day, He works through His followers, through their "hearts." Works are no longer required to prove anything to God, but does that mean we sit back and chill? Nope! Here is what James the "step-brother" of Jesus and a leader of the Jerusalem church said:

Showing Faith

> [14] My brothers and sisters, what good is it if people say they have faith but do nothing to show it? Claiming to have faith can't save anyone, can it? [15] Imagine a brother or sister who is naked and never has enough food to eat. [16] What if one of you said, "Go in peace! Stay warm! Have a nice meal!"? What good is it if you don't actually give them what their body needs? [17] In the same way,

faith is dead when it doesn't result in faithful activity. [18] Someone might claim, "You have faith and I have action." But how can I see your faith apart from your actions? Instead, I'll show you my faith by putting it into practice in faithful action. [19] It's good that you believe that God is one. Ha! Even the demons believe this, and they tremble with fear. [20] Are you so slow? Do you need to be shown that faith without actions has no value at all? [21] What about Abraham, our father? Wasn't he shown to be righteous through his actions when he offered his son Isaac on the altar? [22] See, his faith was at work along with his actions. In fact, his faith was made complete by his faithful actions. [23] So the scripture was fulfilled that says, *Abraham believed God, and God regarded him as righteous* [my italics]. What is more, Abraham was called God's friend. [24] So you see that a person is shown to be righteous through faithful actions and not through faith alone (James 2:14-24, CEB).

I used the *Common English Bible* (CEB) here for two reasons: 1) it is in contemporary English, but matches the older translations in context very well and 2) instead of using the traditional words *deeds* for both the *works* proponent and the *faith* proponent, it uses "faithful activity" for the result of real faith and "action" for the works component. This stresses the difference more. If the person really has faith and is working on increasing it by moving closer to God, it will just naturally result in "faithful activity." If the person is legalistic and not doing it from a "faith-filled" heart, then they will do nothing or only as an "action" out of duty not love. James's statement was, of course, also toward lazy Christians of that day who may have initially accepted Jesus grace and then sat on it and let it shrivel, die, and fall off the Vine. Whether they really ever "heart wise" accepted the Lord, only He knew or knows today; but James is saying that if they really had faith, then they would not be able to help having "faithful activities."

The Apostles and church leaders were already dealing with lazy "Christians" in their day and, unfortunately, some leaders were already leading people off into lazy or even licentious versions of false Christianity. The Gnostics were a group always claiming to be "Christian" and siphoning off Christians from the early church. They taught that the body and the spirit were separate issues and therefore, you didn't have to give up sins of the flesh because what the body did had no effect on the spirits salvation. They believed and taught that even the vilest bodily sins had no effect on salvation because a person's real life was in their spirit only. No works required at all in that group–the ultimate lazy (and fake) "Christianity."

As stated in the chapter on faith and grace, when we draw on God's grace for our faith, we develop our faith and our own grace which then leads us to have compassion (grace) for others. It is always about our relationship with God through the Holy Spirit and Jesus, our Mediator. Without that, we don't have faith. We don't have grace and we don't have "faithful activities" toward others. We will have left the path of the salvation walk.

Visitor's Sunday: Still on Lazy Christianity

Have you ever visited a church where a "country club atmosphere" existed? You walk in and no one greets you or it is only quick and cursory. Prior to services, people are standing around talking to each other in groups, but no one walks over and says hello to you. You find a seat only to be chastised by a couple who come and say, "That's our seat!" Not, "Oh so nice of you to visit our church, we are…." The "country club atmosphere" is a severe form of group laziness. They have no faith left from lack of use, so they have no "faithful activity." They believe that since they did something (action/works) it accomplished something "Christian." They have lost their focus on Jesus Christ. They are no longer walking out their salvation. It is not difficult to do in this busy, goal-oriented culture. Don't let it happen to you.

Although we shouldn't do works, as James says, if we truly have faith in God, we should have, without effort, "faithful activities." These faithful activities are referred to in some translations as "bearing fruit" but I like the way the NLT Bible says it in Romans, "⁴ So, my dear brothers and sisters, this is the point: You died to

81

the power of the law when you died with Christ. And now you are united with the one who was raised from the dead. As a result, we can produce a harvest of good deeds for God" (Romans 7:4, NLT). Well, you ask, "What are these good deeds?" I usually stick to translations, but am going to use an excerpt from the Message Bible which some would call a paraphrase. As the authors of the Message state, "The original books of the Bible were not written in formal language. (Many subsequent Bibles have been translated into "formal" language, not the original "common" tongue.) *The Message* tries to recapture the Word in the words we use today."[xiii] Here is how the Message states it, "[22-23] But what happens when we live God's way? He brings gifts into our lives, much the same way that fruit appears in an orchard—things like affection for others, exuberance about life, serenity. We develop the willingness to stick with things, a sense of compassion in the heart and a conviction that a basic holiness permeates things and people. We find ourselves involved in loyal commitments, not needing to force our way in life, able to marshal and direct our energies wisely" (Galatians 5:22, The Message, MSG). Most translations condense all of that intended expression into a more concise statement like this one, "[22] But the fruit of the Spirit is love, joy, peace, patience, kindness, goodness, faithfulness, [23] gentleness, and self-control. There is no law against things like this" (Galatians 5:22-23, CEB).

So salvation is accepting Jesus Christ as your Savior based upon God's sacrifice of Him on the cross, which is the center point of history. Accept Jesus and you are "saved" and considered a child of God. You have received the indwelling of the Holy Spirit and now must "walk out your salvation" from day to day. To do that you must pray, worship, read the Word, but through all of this, renew your relationship with God through Jesus, day by day. You will make mistakes. It is a given–we are human, but He will forgive every one of them you ask forgiveness for.

Chapter Six

WHAT IS THIS THING CALLED LOVE?

I grew up in the 50s and 60s. Divorce was illegal except for what were considered very good reasons. Until I was 12 years old, my mother and father did not live together. They were "separated." He lived in the city and I saw him so rarely for a while that I hid behind our console television set when he came on my birthday one day with a sack of toys. I didn't know who he was. I was the last of two "litters" (families of kids) by my father. I was born "late" in that my older sisters were planned 4 years apart and I came along unexpectedly 8 years after the last one at time when moms usually don't have kids anymore. I missed out on my family's earlier, happier years.

We were poor, but as a kid I didn't know that; and we had family issues. I wasn't physically abused. In fact, once I grew up and found out what others had gone through, I figured that I had not had it bad at all. By the time I came along there was a major ingredient in healthy families that was terribly missing in ours–love, family love, love of parents to child, child to parents, siblings to siblings. I am sure it was there somewhere, but it was never expressed. Children need to know verbally that they are loved. Neglect would be the best description of my upbringing. It wasn't intentional, just circumstantial would be the way to say it. It also seemed to be a cultural norm for that era. People, even among relatives, did not verbally express love for one another. Maybe it was the horrible losses of WWII and the Korean War. So, I did what most neglected or otherwise abused kids do–I learned to manipulate my environment and people to protect myself and obtain my desired outcomes. I also developed a lot of pent up anger that I carried and unfortunately exhibited on occasion until God helped me in that area.

Even when I met my wife in college, I didn't love her as I know love now. I liked her and she met the mental list of requirements I had developed for a happy family. She met my criteria to make a great wife and mom. That is all I wanted from life at that point–a happy family like those I saw on 50s and 60s television. Like I thought all my friends and acquaintances had. When I started walking the Christian life, I began to learn what love really was, and it wasn't manipulating people to get my way, or expecting people to meet certain criteria I had developed or they couldn't be my friends. I began to really love my wife and my kids as they came along.

We had been a military family at the beginning of our marriage and had gotten out after the Vietnam War, but in 1979, however, I was recalled to active duty and we were sent to an Air Force Base in (what was then known as) the Federal Republic of Germany (West Germany). The unit I was assigned to was a small helicopter unit that flew higher ranking military officers and, occasionally, government officials up to Cabinet Level around West Germany and surrounding West European countries and England.

When we arrived, the unit (small military organization) was absolutely, repulsively, rampant in hardcore pornography and the behavior and attitudes that went with that. There was only one practicing Christian family in the unit who had been praying for "reinforcements" for some time. My wife and I were the first of a small wave of Christians to be the "salt" and "light" to arrive and begin to create a change in the spiritual ambience of that unit and turn it around.

There was no space on the base, so we were to live "on the economy." In other words, we lived in a local village or city in rented quarters. Most German apartments were rather small and minimally equipped compared to what Americans are used to; however, God stepped in and "miraculously" provided (that was according to non-believer friends who lived in Germany) a brand new American standard apartment in a nearby village. We moved in and, besides the conditions at work, began to experience one of the most miserable years of our lives!

That part of Germany nearly broke a 300-year-old record for yearly precipitation that first year. It rained, misted, snowed, or was foggy for a year–every day! (No exaggeration!) We watched fruit trees across the street fall over because the soil was so wet. Armed Forces Radio broadcast messages daily on how to deal with cabin fever! Mold grew on our walls behind furniture, on the side welts of my flight boots, everywhere. And our kids had strep, asthma, or some other flu bug most of that first year. Hey, God, this isn't supposed to happen to believers–right? (People who have that belief system haven't read their Bibles.)

That is when it happened! 8 or 9 months into this mess, my wife and I were praying in the living room for God's intervention, especially with our kid's illnesses. I went to a higher, more serious level of prayer than was normal for me. And He answered me! That was my first contact, real contact that confirmed that yes there really is a real God! I wasn't being emotional. In my mind, the image was of God putting His right arm around my shoulder to comfort me and I felt Him put His arm around my shoulders! But the real surprise was the sudden feeling of incredible compassion and love that flowed over me! It was way beyond anything I could have imagined. I am still ashamed to say that, because it was so beyond anything I'd ever experienced or imagined, I pulled back from it immediately. Love scared me!

The Apostle Paul and other biblical writers try to express how wonderful God's love for us is, but they don't even come close to the real thing. I am still so ashamed of pulling back instinctively from God's compassionate touch, but I still cannot imagine anything in this life even coming up to even 10 percent of that same level of love. It cannot be described in human terms! God's love for us is why He had a plan after man's fall in the Garden of Eden to return mankind to a status where they could commune with Him. It is why, "in the fullness of time" that the Messiah prophecied throughout the Old Testament would come and pay the price for our sin, die, be entombed, rise from the dead and return to Heaven to be our Advocate to Father God. In his letter to the Ephesian Church, Paul stated:

> When I think of the wisdom and scope of God's plan, I fall to my knees and pray to the Father, [15]the Creator of everything in heaven and on earth. [16]I pray that from his glorious, unlimited resources he will give you mighty inner strength through his Holy Spirit. [17]And I pray that Christ will be more and more at home in your hearts as you trust in him. May your roots go down deep into the soil of God's marvelous love. [18]And may you have the power to understand, as all God's people should, how wide, how long, how high, and how deep his love really is. *[19]May you experience the love of Christ, though it is so great you will never fully understand it* [my italics]. Then you will be filled with the fullness of life and power that comes from God (Ephesians 3:14-19, NLT).

I love the way that Paul describes, or attempts to describe, God's incredible love for mankind. "Inconceivable[4]" is the word for "you will never fully understand it." And it is true–God's love truly is inconceivable! He is saying that through our cooperation with the indwelling of the Holy Spirit, Jesus the Messiah will be able to be at home in our hearts and then, we will really know the fullness of God's love for His children and we will be made complete in Him! In the book of Romans, Paul says this about the love of Jesus (and therefore the Father):

> [35]Can anything separate us from the love Christ has for us? Can troubles or problems or sufferings or hunger or nakedness or danger or violent death? [36]As it is written in the Scriptures: "For you we

---

4   "Inconceivable" is probably one of the most popular (and short) quotes from one of the most quotable films in the last several decades, "Princess Bride" directed by Rob Reiner and released September 25, 1987. Used repeatedly by a villain in the film called Vizzini, the word is etched in his voice in the minds of all those families that watched it dozens of times together laughing the whole time.

are in danger of death all the time. People think we are worth no more than sheep to be killed" (Psalm 44:22).

[37] But in all these things we are completely victorious through God who showed his love for us. [38] Yes, I am sure that neither death, nor life, nor angels, nor ruling spirits, nothing now, nothing in the future, no powers, [39] nothing above us, nothing below us, nor anything else in the whole world will ever be able to separate us from the love of God that is in Christ Jesus our Lord (Romans 8:35-39, NCV).

The Apostle John in his Gospel (his Good News book), says it this way,"[16] For God so loved the world, that he gave his only begotten Son, that whosoever believeth in him should not perish, but have everlasting life" (John 3:16, KJV). This is probably the most quoted and memorized scripture from the Word because it sums up the whole story of mankind's fall from grace and God's plan to redeem mankind. We hear, memorize and teach John 3:16 so often that many people become desensitized to what it really means. This act of God was the supreme example of agape love: sacrificial love, supreme love, extreme love, the total Love of God!

Jesus crucifixion was the central point of history as far as Christianity is concerned because it was His death, burial and resurrection which enabled mere human beings who sincerely believe in God to receive and experience His Love! Without the connection of the Holy Spirit whom Jesus sent after He returned to Heaven (see John 14:26 and 16:7) only a few people of the Old Testament got to experience it, and only because their hearts were tuned to God. They were not perfect in all other ways, by any means, but God loved them because of their intense love for Him. A. W. Tozer in *The Pursuit of God* had this to say about that, "Now set over against this almost any Bible character who honestly tried to glorify God in his earthly walk. See how God winked at weaknesses and overlooked failures as He poured upon His servants grace and blessing untold. Let it be Abraham, Jacob, David, Daniel, Elijah or whom you will; honor followed honor as harvest the seed. The man of God set his heart to exalt God above all; God accepted his intention as fact and acted accordingly. Not perfection, but holy intention made the difference."[xiv]

It amazes me still, that many people elevate some of these characters or some modern Christian personalities almost to "Godhood." This only leads to their disillusionment when, especially with living saints, they discover they are fallible! Jesus knows we are fallible and that is why one of His "job descriptions" is Advocate, Defense Attorney, between us and God the Father. He serves as the "filter" for a saint's sinfulness, so that the Father does not see it. We are not perfect and we are not going to be perfect until after Jesus comes back! So, get over yourself, God loves you even if you fail! To be honest, most of my failures have come when I either refused to listen to, or didn't stop to ask the Holy Spirit's advice. That is why He is also called the "counselor." His advice comes "straight from the top" literally! This is yet another way that God shows His Love for us, by giving us life advice individually. And another reason that Christianity is not a "religion."

What Types of Love Are in the Bible?

There are four Greek words used for love in the New Testament of the Bible. *Eros* is sensual/sexual love. *Storge* is not specifically used but referred to many times in context; it means family love. *Philia* means brotherly love, the type of love most people exhibit for friends in their lives. Remember in your history lessons that Philadelphia was named that because it was the city of "brotherly love" (philia love, not eros love). *Agape* is the fourth one and the most important, because it is an extraordinary kind of love. It goes beyond what most of us are capable of feeling on our own. It is totally unselfish love and we are typically selfish to at least some degree. But God isn't and He sent Jesus as a human example of this type of love for the rest of us to copy.

During the Charismatic Renewal of the 70s and early 80s, agape love was on everyone's mind. Agape love is the love that Jesus preached. Agape is selfless, sacrificial, unconditional love, the highest of the four types of love in the Bible.[xv]

During the Renewal, agape love was preached, it was sung and was heralded in a hundred different ways; but then, as so often happens, people got side-tracked onto the "creation" again instead of the Creator. They took off on tangents on prosperity, gifts, tongues and other things that were merely shadows of the key issue of Christian living–agape love.

The apostle to the early Gentile churches, Paul was dealing with this problem shortly after these churches inception. It's human nature. Although these things are important, in context with the Word, they are "side issues." In a letter to the Colossian Church, the Apostle Paul said, "[17]These are a shadow of the things that were to come; the reality, however, is found in Christ" (Colossians 2:17, NIV).

Now, finally, there seems to be same reawakening to the "first love" that many churches, just like the Ephesian Church of Revelation, had left (see Revelation 2:1-7). They were busy little bees, doing God's work, tolerating no phonies, but missing the mark entirely. We need to focus on our relationship to Jesus. If we don't, we can miss it also. While writing this chapter, I was looking through some old journaling notes and came across this note:

> 4-24-2000, 11:15pm: Was not able to go to sleep and was praying to God about loving Him and wanting to be able to love people like He does, when He told me—"Eternal life is not the ultimate reward for the Christian. It is a wonderful thing, but the real reward for the Christian is spending eternity in His presence, in His Glory." (For God is Love!)

The unsaved will also inherit eternal life, but it will be without hope, without love, without God's presence. Man seeks love throughout his physical life (usually in all the wrong places) when what he is really seeking is God's love and approval. This Love of God is what makes life complete. This is why a Christian believer may be living in abject poverty and persecution in communist or some Islamic countries or living in relatively safe luxury in America and be happy in their devotion to the Lord—because they are living in God's love.

The unsaved are never really happy, because you cannot have true "happiness" without God's love which produces God's peace, which produces joy, hope and love toward others in our lives.

But how does one get this type of happiness? He gets it by seeking God himself. As Tommy Tenney says in "God Chasers" you must seek God's face and not His hands. In our materialist society, too many Christians, pastors, evangelists and churches are seeking the benefits of God either on a higher priority or equal priority with God's presence. A. W. Tozer spoke of this phenomena when he wrote, "When religion has said its last word, there is little that we need other than God Himself. The evil habit of seeking *God-and* [my italics] effectively prevents us from finding God in full revelation. In the "and" lies our great woe. If we omit the "and" we shall soon find God, and in Him we shall find that for which we have all our lives been secretly longing.[xvi]

God's manifest presence is what it is all about. Everything else does not matter without seeking His presence. Again, that is why a Christian living a persecuted existence in a stronghold of anti-Christian spiritual forces in some ways has an advantage in seeking God's presence than the safely ensconced (usually Western) Christian. As Paul says in his letter to the Ephesian Church, "[7]The end of the world is coming soon. Therefore, be earnest and disciplined in your prayers. [8]Most important of all, continue to show deep love for each other, for love covers a multitude of sins. [9]Cheerfully share your home with those who need a meal or a place to stay" (1 Peter 4:7-9, NLT).

God works through natural means, for the most part, until His presence becomes so powerful (through the prayers and intercession of the saints) that He parts seas, defeats armies, burns mountains, holds back rivers and collapses enormous fortifications for His peoples' benefit. The Israelites left Egyptian slavery with all the wealth of the Egyptians. All the wealth of the evil cultures they (through God) conquered was transferred to the Israelites. Later emissaries of various nations willingly brought wealth to Israel as gifts (and sometimes somewhat unwillingly as tribute) all due to God's love upon that nation and its early rulers. But time and time again throughout their history, when their focus shifted to the benefits rather than their provider, they fell into depravity and finally were conquered and enslaved. If they had kept their hearts in love with God rather than His benefits package, they would have remained a nation throughout history!

So the real answer to human need is the Love of God. Do you really love God (Jesus, the Father, and the Holy Spirit) or are you just playing the "Christian yuppie game" hoping to derive YOUR hearts desires through a relationship to God. Scripture says that God knows your mind, but a wise father never continues to give gifts to a greedy, selfish child. He knows that it will only drive the child further into rebellion and avarice and further from his love.

God is the ultimate wise Father and He KNOWS what is in our hearts, whether it is love for Him or desire for THINGS through Him. In the book of Matthew, Jesus is quoted as saying, "[32]The people who don't know God keep trying to get these things, and your Father in Heaven knows you need them. [33] Seek first God's kingdom and what God wants. Then all your other needs will be met as well (Matthew 6:32-33, NCV).

The really important things that you can have no matter what your situation in the world are the ones the Apostle Paul describes in the love chapter of Corinthians—love, peace, joy (hope comes out of these). Rather than put the whole of 1 Corinthians 13 (the "love chapter") in the book, I recommend that you pull out, open up, or bring up (eBooks) your favorite Bible and read it. If you don't have a Bible, but have a smartphone, computer, or other electronic device, just Google the word Bible and there is a wealth of great Bible websites. Amazon Kindle and others eBook retailers have app's for every device with which you have access to dozens of translations of the Christian Bible. Read it in several translations and paraphrases if possible. Pray about God's love and let God minister to you about it. God is Love, the very manifestation and embodiment of it. Seek Him, seek His Presence, go beyond the anointing into His Glory and you will comprehend.

Love and Trust Are Not Synonymous!

At this point, there is a something that needs to be said. Loving people and trusting them are not the same thing! This is not something I've ever read or heard taught except in context with a specific scripture and a "revelation" that came with reading it a few years ago. Too many Christians have a "Pollyanna" idea that they must be "honest and carefree" with people no matter what the circumstance. In that scripture the Apostle John said, "[23]Because of the miraculous signs Jesus did in Jerusalem at the Passover celebration, many began to trust in him. [24] But Jesus didn't trust them, because he knew human nature. [25] No one needed to tell him what mankind is really like" (John 2:23-25, NLT). This is not "mean-spirited." This is reality.

Jesus said some very realistic things as when He said, [6] "Don't waste what is holy on people who are unholy. Don't throw your pearls to pigs! They will trample the pearls, then turn and attack you" (Matthew 7:6, NLT). In another similar statement about not being the foolish "Pollyanna" type Christian (been there, done that, won't do again– I hope!) He said, "[16] "Look, I am sending you out as sheep among wolves. So be as shrewd as snakes and harmless as doves" (Matthew 10:16, NLT). People frequently take advantage of Christians on purpose. Some of them purport to be Christians themselves and use their knowledge of a few verses about benevolence to coerce, through scripture, favors which they really don't deserve. (Their heart is not on Jesus, it is on getting their way.) This is another of those "balance" things. Yes, we are supposed to be benevolent, more so than worldly people, but we need to use some of the "common sense" that God gives us through the Holy Spirit. Sometimes, you have to practice "tough love" with "Christians" who live to take advantage of others.

Jesus put on human flesh, grew up as a man, worked for years as a carpenter (probably smashed a finger or thumb with a hammer a few times and was tempted to say bad things), (because He) suffered every temptation common to mankind, and voluntarily died of crucifixion (still one of the cruelest of executions) because He loved mankind enough to do that to give mankind a way back to God!

But He also knew how treacherous man can be, even unintentionally. Many Christians, including myself, have made the "American altruistic" mistake of equating love and trust and been "hurt" physically, emotionally, spiritually, or financially. Often this has happened as the Holy Spirit was trying to tell that individual (in some cases me) to stop what they were doing or about to do. You'd warn your children!

Occasionally, that "nagging" by the Holy Spirit may come when you are writing or emailing something to someone you "trust" or about to tell them something that you just think they need to know. (Or these days, you may be about to put something on social media.) You feel you "must" do this because you are a Christian. You may be conveying some information to help out others who have asked you to be their spokesman. Not all things that seem appropriate, honest things to do, etc. are a good idea! Some are a very bad idea! But there is One who knows whether something should be communicated, or not, by you to a particular someone or group–the Holy Spirit. God knows people's hearts and because of this, He has the "big picture" or "view from the top" as some say. If the Holy Spirit is nagging you to stop–STOP! Delete it. Burn or shred it. Forget it. Disappoint those who asked you to be their spokesman. But don't deliver it!

The Holy Spirit knows everything that is going on and you don't. You don't know what the effect of your input (in trust) is going to have. The absolutely worst on-the-job mistake I ever made, a major professional setback, was because I communicated (in being an honest Christian and helping other subordinates) to a "Christian" supervisor while under pressure from the Spirit not to do it! Listen to the Spirit. Don't make the same mistake. Love the sinner, the other Christian and even your enemy, but show wisdom and realize they are different in more ways from you than is "on the surface." Complete, unabated, trust is something to reserve for God, family, and absolute best and proven friends. And even then, aside from God, listen to the Spirit first. This is the opposite of the saying, "Open mouth, insert foot." Instead you should, "Close mouth, ask God." God will help you (and me) keep our feet out of our mouths! Just ask. We can always trust Him.

[4] Love is patient and kind. Love is not jealous or boastful or proud [5] or rude. It does not demand its own way. It is not irritable, and it keeps no record of being wronged. [6] It does not rejoice about injustice but rejoices whenever the truth wins out. [7] Love never gives up, never loses faith, is always hopeful, and endures through every circumstance (1 Corinthians 13:4-7, NLT).

[13] Three things will last forever—faith, hope, and love—and the greatest of these is love (1 Corinthians 13:13, NLT).

Chapter Seven

WHAT IS ALL THIS RESURRECTION BUSINESS ABOUT?

⸻

M any years ago when I was working in a boy's camping ministry, I had a young man tell me that his father had informed him that Jesus was not really resurrected from the dead. His father, though attending a Christian church, had not given up many of the beliefs of his birth family's original religion–The Church of Jesus Christ of the Latter Day Saints—commonly called the Mormons. They are good people, but they do not believe the same way Biblical Christians do about the Godhead. In fact, they believe our Christian Church apostacized away millennia ago. I won't cover the differences here, but if you want to understand the differences please read Dr. Walter Martin's information on it in his book *The Kingdom of the Cults*. They may not believe the same as Biblical Christians do, but we have freedom of religion in the USA, so there will be no condemnation about their beliefs in this book.

The problem with this revelation by the boy concerned was what could I tell him since it would be going against what his father was teaching him? I decided to follow God's Word and tell him the truth from the Bible, specifically from the Apostle Paul's first letter to the Corinthian believers in chapter 15. The Apostle Paul was a brilliant man, so as the Apostle Peter mentions in one of his letters, he is a little hard to follow sometimes. So, read it slowly and then read it again. Read it in several translations and/or paraphrases to get the full impact. This scripture is central to Christianity. If you think it is something modern about people distorting the gospel, think again. In Paul's time, deceivers were already distorting the good news. That is what he is dealing with in this part of his letter:

> [12] "If we preach that Christ was raised from death, how can some of you say that the dead will not be raised to life? [13] If they won't be raised to life, Christ himself wasn't raised to life. [14] And if Christ wasn't raised to life, our message is worthless, and so is your faith. [15] If the dead won't be raised to life, we have told lies about God by saying that he raised Christ to life, when he really did not. [16] "So if the dead won't be raised to life, Christ wasn't raised to life. [17] Unless Christ was raised to life, your faith is useless, and you are still living in your sins. [18] And those people who died after putting their faith in him are completely lost. [19] If our hope in Christ is good only for this life, we are worse off than anyone else. [20] "But Christ has been raised to life! And he makes us certain that others will also be raised to life. [21] Just as we will die because of Adam, we will be raised to life because of Christ. [22] Adam brought death to all of us, and Christ will bring life to all of us. [23] But we must each wait our turn. Christ was the first to be raised to life, and his people will be raised to life when he returns" (1 Corinthians 15:12-23, CEV).

When he keeps saying, "Raised to life", he is not referring to just a spiritual life. If a human body cannot be resurrected from death, even after decomposition or destruction, then what is the point of being a Christian? We are not just promised life in Heaven after death, but a real body (albeit a bit different from this one) upon Jesus's return in the future. Jesus's resurrection, by the way, was not the first, but it was dramatically different in a very important way in which we will discuss shortly. There are a several resurrections recorded in the Old

Testament. Two are very similar. One is highly unusual, but involves the second prophet after he is long dead.

Old Testament Resurrections

The first involves the prophet Elijah. Elijah is one of the most prominent prophets or as theologians refer to him and several others–Major Prophets. In case you haven't read that story, or it has been awhile, here is a short synopsis of what leads up to this resurrection miracle.

Elijah appears suddenly on the scene in the 17th chapter of 1 Kings in opposition to two of the most infamous, evil rulers of Israel in those times–Ahab and Jezebel. The first thing God has him do is prophecy a three and one-half year severe drought for the region due to how evil the people have become. During the famine that follows the drought's effects, he is travelling through the town of Zarephath where he encounters a destitute widow who is preparing the last little bit of her flour and olive oil for a small meal for her and her son. She and her son are destined to die from starvation after that. He asks her to prepare it for him instead. Wow! How arrogant does that seem! But this is not human arrogance. It is a test of faith on the woman's part. She knows Elijah is the Prophet of God to Israel, as unpopular as he may be because of the drought. (There is a sermon somewhere in that.) Elijah promised her (prophecied) that her barrel of meal (flour) and her container of olive oil would never run out during the rest of the drought and that was exactly what happened.

This woman provided a room for Elijah to stay in when he was passing through. One day her son sickens and dies. Elijah is in town and here is the miracle of resurrection:

Elijah Brings a Boy Back to Life

> [17] Several days later, the son of the woman who owned the house got sick, and he kept getting worse, until finally he died.[18] The woman shouted at Elijah, "What have I done to you? I thought

you were God's prophet. Did you come here to cause the death of my son as a reminder that I've sinned against God?"[19] "Bring me your son," Elijah said. Then he took the boy from her arms and carried him upstairs to the room where he was staying. Elijah laid the boy on his bed [20] and prayed, "Lord God, why did you do such a terrible thing to this woman? She's letting me stay here, and now you've let her son die." [21] Elijah stretched himself out over the boy three times, while praying, "Lord God, bring this boy back to life!"

[22] The Lord answered Elijah's prayer, and the boy started breathing again. [23] Elijah picked him up and carried him downstairs. He gave the boy to his mother and said, "Look, your son is alive."[24] "You are God's prophet!" the woman replied. "Now I know that you really do speak for the Lord" (1 Kings 17:17-24, CEV).

Notice the woman's very typical human reaction to the trauma of her son's death in verse eighteen. A reminder of her sins? Stuff happens. It happens to Christians as it happened to her, a Jewish believer. We have a very special relationship with God through the New Covenant, but things will still happen, but God's infinite love can overcome and He restores her son through Elijah's intervention.

Elijah's disciple that replaced him in his prophet-to-Israel capacity when Elijah was taken up into Heaven was Elisha. When first studying the Bible, sometimes people get confused between the two. Not only were they closely associated, but names were similar and some of the episodes in their prophetic lives were almost identical. This is Elisha's resurrection miracle many years later. Like his mentor, Elijah, Elisha had been given a room to stay in by a wealthy couple along the route he took through the area. In return for her kindness, he prophecied she would have a son (her husband and her were childless) and she bore a son the next year. Time passed and the son grew old enough to go out to the fields to see his dad. Elisha was still receiving room and board in the home on his travels through the area when her son got an illness which led quickly to his death. Elisha was over at Mount Carmel, about a day's walk away. This is what she did:

> [24] She saddled the donkey and said to her servant, "Let's go. And don't slow down unless I tell you to." [25] She left at once for Mount Carmel to talk with Elisha. When Elisha saw her coming, he said, "Gehazi, look! It's the woman from Shunem. [26] Run and meet her. And ask her if everything is all right with her and her family." "Everything is fine," she answered Gehazi. [27] But as soon as she got to the top of the mountain, she went over and grabbed Elisha by the feet. Gehazi started toward her to push her away, when Elisha said, "Leave her alone! Don't you see how sad she is? But the Lord hasn't told me why."
>
> [28] The woman said, "Sir, I begged you not to get my hopes up, and I didn't even ask you for a son."
>
> [29] "Gehazi, get ready and go to her house," Elisha said. "Take along my walking stick, and when you get there, lay it on the boy's face. Don't stop to talk to anyone, even if they try to talk to you."
>
> [30] But the boy's mother said to Elisha, "I swear by the living Lord and by your own life that I won't leave without you." So Elisha got up and went with them.
>
> [31] Gehazi ran on ahead and laid Elisha's walking stick on the boy's face, but the boy didn't move or make a sound. Gehazi ran back to Elisha and said, "The boy didn't wake up."
>
> [32] Elisha arrived at the woman's house and went straight to his room, where he saw the boy's body on his bed. [33] He walked in, shut the door, and prayed to the Lord. [34] Then he got on the bed and stretched out over the dead body, with his mouth on the boy's mouth, his eyes on his eyes, and his hand on his hands. As he laid there, the boy's body became warm. [35] Elisha got up and

walked back and forth in the room, and then he went back and leaned over the boy's body. The boy sneezed seven times and opened his eyes.

[36] Elisha called out to Gehazi, "Have the boy's mother come here." Gehazi did, and when she was at the door, Elisha said, "You can take your son" (2 Kings 4:24-36, CEV).

Notice the first thing she does when she encounters Elisha. She prostrates herself before the man of God and grabs his feet. She is not going to let him go anywhere except to her house to heal her son! She will not give up and when he tells his servant, Gehazi, to take his walking stick and place it on the boy to heal him, she absolutely will not settle for that either. This principle of "never give up" in your appeals to God is represented here in two translations:

Effective Prayer

> [7] Keep on asking, and you will receive what you ask for. Keep on seeking, and you will find. Keep on knocking, and the door will be opened to you (Matthew 7:7, NLT).

The King James Version says it this way:

> [7] Ask, and it shall be given you; seek, and ye shall find; knock, and it shall be opened unto you: (Matthew 7:7, KJV)

Contrary to our modern craving for instant gratification, we are not to give up if we do not get an answer from God right away. As some put it, "God has His own timing." The implication is there in the *King James Version* as in several others that this is a continuing process (seek and you shall find), but it is left to the reader to figure it out through context. The *New Living Translation* and other contemporary translations bring out the implied (by context and idiom) message which is very helpful, especially to a new student to the Bible. Here, in an account in the Old Testament we see the principle that Jesus says in the New Testament–persevere in prayer! She persevered with God's representative and she got her son back.

The last recorded resurrection in the Old Testament dealt with Elisha again long after he was dead and in a tomb. Some background first. When Elijah told Elisha that he was going away (being taken up to Heaven) he asked him how he could bless him as he was taking over Elijah's responsibilities. They had just crossed the Jordan River on dry land by Elijah striking the water with his cloak and the crossing the river on dry riverbed. (Moses and the Israelite nation had crossed the Jordon on dry land many years before when the feet of the priests carrying the Ark of the Covenant touched the water.) This is how Elisha became the prophet of God:

> [9]After they had reached the other side, Elijah said, "Elisha, the Lord will soon take me away. What can I do for you before that happens?"
> Elisha answered, "Please give me twice as much of your power as you give the other prophets, so I can be the one who takes your place as their leader."
> [10]"It won't be easy," Elijah answered. "It can happen only if you see me as I am being taken away."
> [11]Elijah and Elisha were walking along and talking, when suddenly there appeared between them a flaming chariot pulled by fiery horses. Right away, a strong wind took Elijah up into heaven. [12]Elisha saw this and shouted, "Israel's cavalry and chariots have taken my master away!" After Elijah had gone, Elisha tore his clothes in sorrow (2 Kings 2:9-12, CEV).

From that point in time Elisha, with a double portion of Elijah's anointed power, took over Elijah's ministry duties to Israel. After many years, he died and was buried in a tomb. The author of 2 Kings relates, "[20]"Elisha died and was buried. Every year in the spring, Moab's leaders sent raiding parties into Israel. [21] Once, while some Israelites were burying a man's body, they saw a group of Moabites. The Israelites quickly threw the body into Elisha's tomb and ran away. As soon as the man's body touched the bones of Elisha, the man came back to life and stood up" (2 Kings 13:20-2, CEV).

Although most people associate the claim that someone can send someone an article like a handkerchief that has been "anointed" by a "servant of God" for a donation and they can apply it and be healed with scams, there are a few instances in the Bible where the anointing is on something inanimate and can heal. Elisha's bones are the Old Testament example. In the New Testament, after Jesus had returned to Heaven and the Apostles were healing people and working miracles some similar things happened. In the book of Acts, the author Luke states, "[11] God gave Paul the power to work great miracles. [12] People even took handkerchiefs and aprons that had touched Paul's body, and they carried them to everyone who was sick. All of the sick people were healed, and the evil spirits went out" (Acts 19:11-12, CEV). Healing is based upon faith not the object which is only a "point of contact" for the faithful. The object used does not heal; the Spirit of God does through the faith of those involved. (And it doesn't say Paul asked for any donations for the healing.)

Those are the three recorded resurrections of the Old Testament. There are three resurrections in the New Testament accomplished by Jesus and two by His apostles Peter and Paul. Although some theologically minded people try to assert that these were just for "signs" I don't buy that. Especially if you read your Bible in contemporary language, your mother tongue, you begin to see that many of the miracles He did were because of His compassion for hurting people. If we are to believe the writings in the Bible, He is the representation of God's Love for mankind. He wasn't just going around "filling squares" so some modern theologian or "expert" on the Bible can show how each of these events proved He was the Messiah fulfilling prophecy.

He was far more than just fulfilling prophecies; He was fulfilling God's Love. The first recorded resurrection by Jesus is in the book of Luke and Luke relates:

"[11] Soon afterward Jesus went with his disciples to the village of Nain, and a large crowd followed him. [12] A funeral procession was coming out as he approached the village gate. The young man who had died was a widow's only son, and a large crowd from the village was with her. [13] When the Lord saw her, his heart overflowed with compassion. "Don't cry!" he said. [14] Then he walked over to the coffin and touched it, and the bearers stopped. "Young man," he said, "I tell you, get up." [15] Then the dead boy sat up and began to talk! And Jesus gave him back to his mother" (Luke 7:11-15, NLT).

In verse thirteen, it says, "His heart overflowed with compassion." He was not looking for ways to give the Israelites more signs. In fact, He reprimanded them for demanding signs that He was the Messiah. *He healed out of love.* In the case of this widow, there were no government programs to take care of destitute people, only the family, and this was her only son who would have been her financial support in her old age. Jewish widows without family were often destitute unless they were young enough to remarry. The support of qualified widows was one of the first benevolence programs the Christian church established. The Apostles set up a system through the deacons of the church for caring for Christian widows who had no support or means.

The second resurrection by Jesus is related in the book of Matthew. Matthew relates the story:

[18] As Jesus was saying this, the leader of a synagogue came and knelt before him. "My daughter has just died," he said, "but you can bring her back to life again if you just come and lay your hand on her."
[19] So Jesus and his disciples got up and went with him. [23] When Jesus arrived at the official's home, he saw the noisy crowd and heard the funeral music. [24] "Get out!" he told them. "The girl isn't

dead; she's only asleep." But the crowd laughed at him. [25] After the crowd was put outside, however, Jesus went in and took the girl by the hand, and she stood up! [26] The report of this miracle swept through the entire countryside (Matthew 9:18-19, 23-26, NLT).

These people had not been dead long. In our times, people are revived often right after they die externally. This didn't happen in those days. Decomposition began immediately, so burials were basically right away. Still a person might think that since these had just died it might not have been a miracle. The person was somehow accidently revived. But the last recorded resurrection by Jesus leaves no doubt about the restorative power involved. This one was for a sign, not just compassion. This was Jesus friend Lazarus. Jesus intentionally waited for several days after He heard that Lazarus was very ill. This was unusual for Him, especially for this favored friend and his sisters, Mary and Martha. He had often been their guest. So, when He arrived in Bethany where Lazarus had lived and was now entombed, Lazarus had been dead for four days. That is not like reviving someone who has just drowned or just had a heart attack. His body had started serious decomposition in that period of time. This is a bit long quotation, but to remove any "unrelated" verses would make it choppy. This is the whole story of the resurrection of Lazarus:

The Death of Lazarus

11 A man named Lazarus was sick. He lived in the town of Bethany, where Mary and her sister Martha lived. [2] Mary was the woman who later put perfume on the Lord and wiped his feet with her hair. Mary's brother was Lazarus, the man who was now sick. [3] So Mary and Martha sent someone to tell Jesus, "Lord, the one you love is sick."

[4] When Jesus heard this, he said, "This sickness will not end in death. It is for the glory of God, to bring glory to the Son of God."

[5] Jesus loved Martha and her sister and Lazarus. [6] But when he

heard that Lazarus was sick, he stayed where he was for two more days. [7] Then Jesus said to his followers, "Let's go back to Judea." [8] The followers said, "But Teacher, some people there tried to stone you to death only a short time ago. Now you want to go back there?"

[9] Jesus answered, "Are there not twelve hours in the day? If anyone walks in the daylight, he will not stumble, because he can see by this world's light. [10] But if anyone walks at night, he stumbles because there is no light to help him see."

[11] After Jesus said this, he added, "Our friend Lazarus has fallen asleep, but I am going there to wake him."

[12] The followers said, "But Lord, if he is only asleep, he will be all right."

[13] Jesus meant that Lazarus was dead, but his followers thought he meant Lazarus was really sleeping. [14] So then Jesus said plainly, "Lazarus is dead. [15] And I am glad for your sakes I was not there so that you may believe. But let's go to him now."

[16] Then Thomas (the one called Didymus) said to the other followers, "Let us also go so that we can die with him."

Jesus in Bethany

[17] When Jesus arrived, he learned that Lazarus had already been dead and in the tomb for four days. [18] Bethany was about two miles from Jerusalem. [19] Many of the Jews had come there to comfort Martha and Mary about their brother.

[20] When Martha heard that Jesus was coming, she went out to meet him, but Mary stayed home. [21] Martha said to Jesus, "Lord, if you had been here, my brother would not have died. [22] But I know that even now God will give you anything you ask."

[23] Jesus said, "Your brother will rise and live again."

²⁴ Martha answered, "I know that he will rise and live again in the resurrection on the last day."

²⁵ Jesus said to her, "I am the resurrection and the life. Those who believe in me will have life even if they die. ²⁶ And everyone who lives and believes in me will never die. Martha, do you believe this?"

²⁷ Martha answered, "Yes, Lord. I believe that you are the Christ, the Son of God, the One coming to the world."

Jesus Cries

²⁸ After Martha said this, she went back and talked to her sister Mary alone. Martha said, "The Teacher is here and he is asking for you." ²⁹ When Mary heard this, she got up quickly and went to Jesus. ³⁰ Jesus had not yet come into the town but was still at the place where Martha had met him. ³¹ The Jews were with Mary in the house, comforting her. When they saw her stand and leave quickly, they followed her, thinking she was going to the tomb to cry there.

³² But Mary went to the place where Jesus was. When she saw him, she fell at his feet and said, "Lord, if you had been here, my brother would not have died."

³³ When Jesus saw Mary crying and the Jews who came with her also crying, he was upset and was deeply troubled. ³⁴ He asked, "Where did you bury him?"

"Come and see, Lord," they said.

³⁵ Jesus cried.

³⁶ So the Jews said, "See how much he loved him."

³⁷ But some of them said, "If Jesus opened the eyes of the blind man, why couldn't he keep Lazarus from dying?"

Jesus Raises Lazarus

[38] Again feeling very upset, Jesus came to the tomb. It was a cave with a large stone covering the entrance. [39] Jesus said, "Move the stone away."

Martha, the sister of the dead man, said, "But, Lord, it has been four days since he died. There will be a bad smell."

[40] Then Jesus said to her, "Didn't I tell you that if you believed you would see the glory of God?"

[41] So they moved the stone away from the entrance. Then Jesus looked up and said, "Father, I thank you that you heard me. [42] I know that you always hear me, but I said these things because of the people here around me. I want them to believe that you sent me." [43] After Jesus said this, he cried out in a loud voice, "Lazarus, come out!" [44] The dead man came out, his hands and feet wrapped with pieces of cloth, and a cloth around his face.

Jesus said to them, "Take the cloth off of him and let him go" (John 11:1-44, NCV).

As far as we know, this was the last resurrection accomplished by Jesus. There are two recorded resurrections done by Peter (see Acts 9:36-42) and Paul (see Acts 20:9-12). At the moment of Jesus death on the cross, it was reported that many believers spontaneously resurrected and walked around Jerusalem (see Matthew 27:52-53). However, all of these resurrections, both before and after Jesus death, burial and resurrection were not the same kind of resurrection. One of the reasons I wanted to write this book is that, like many Christians, I received little or no discipling on what some of the scriptures in the Bible meant. I remember, many years ago, coming across the following verses: [21] "For since by man came death, by man came also the resurrection of the dead. [22] For as in Adam all die, even so in Christ shall all be made alive. [23] But every man in his own order: Christ the firstfruits; afterward they that are Christ's at his coming" (1 Corinthians 15:21-23, KJV). Until I studied it for a while, I couldn't understand why He could be the first when lots of others had been resurrected before Him. They are "apples and oranges" as an old friend used to say to me. They are not the same miracle.

I used the *King James Version* here because this is one of those times that it is a little more accurate in that it uses the phrase "Christ the firstfruits." This is an old term that means the first produce of the harvest which was normally given as a sacrifice to God at the temple. Many other translations drop this term except for the New Living Translation which says, "Christ was raised as the first of the harvest...." This idea of "harvest" is very important. Jesus was both a sacrifice and the first to be resurrected in a "glorified body."

Jesus resurrection, as I already mentioned, and the resurrection of "all who belong to Christ" upon His return are not the same as the bodily resurrections we have already read about. Not even close! All those people died physically once again. In the interim time, they had illnesses, aches and pains and suffered the usual maladies of aging. Jesus and those that follow will not! And they will never die again! Those are the promises of being "Christian"– we go to Heaven when we die (our spirit and soul) and then will receive new spiritual (and material) bodies when Jesus Christ returns.

But Jesus will never die again, and neither will we, after our earthly death and the resurrection, if we are His followers. Our bodies will be like His body– glorified and both spiritual and physical. *There had never been a glorified body until Jesus came back from the dead,* but all Christians will have glorified bodies after the resurrections of the Book of Revelation. Paul goes on to say: "[52] It will happen suddenly, quicker than the blink of an eye. At the sound of the last trumpet the dead will be raised. We will all be changed, so that we will never die again. [53] Our dead and decaying bodies will be changed into bodies that won't die or decay" (1 Corinthians 15:52-53, CEV).

Jesus, during the 40 days He fellowshipped with His apostles and disciples after His resurrection knew that people would try to say He was only a spirit after His death. He made a point from the first few days to rectify this. On the day of Jesus resurrection, Peter had gone to the empty tomb after Mary's report to the Apostles. The Word says he returned to where the Apostles were staying and then talks about two of "them" (apparently by context two, one of which was an Apostle, or they were with the Apostles) walked to Emmaus 7 miles distant from Jerusalem. A "stranger" fell in with them along the way and at their invitation had supper with them. After eating solid food with them, he reminded them of all the prophecies of His death and resurrection. As they suddenly saw Him as He was, He disappeared. They quickly returned to Jerusalem to tell the other Apostles they had seen the Lord. This is how Luke reports it:

> [35] Then they told what had happened on the road, and how he was known to them in the breaking of the bread.
>
> Jesus Appears to His Disciples
>
> [36] As they were talking about these things, Jesus himself stood among them, and said to them, "Peace to you!" [37] But they were startled and frightened and thought they saw a spirit. [38] And he said to them, "Why are you troubled, and why do doubts arise in your hearts? [39] See my hands and my feet, that it is I myself. Touch me, and see. For a spirit does not have flesh and bones as you see that I have." [40] And when he had said this, he showed them his hands and his feet. [41] And while they still disbelieved for joy and were marveling, he said to them, "Have you anything here to eat?" [42] They gave him a piece of broiled fish, [43] and he took it and ate before them (Luke 24:35-42, ESV).

He had them touch His body to see that he wasn't just a spirit (some translations use the word *ghost*) and then asked for and ate solid food in front of them. It would be hard to believe that He wasn't just some ethereal apparition since He had just done the impossible—He had entered the room and their midst without coming through the locked door. He had disappeared at the supper table before two of them in Emmaus. Later He came back again when one of the apostles that wasn't there the first time was now there. This is covered in John's Gospel:

> [24] Now Thomas, one of the Twelve, called the Twin, was not with them when Jesus came. [25] So the other disciples told him, "We have seen the Lord." But he said to them, "Unless I see in his hands the mark of the nails, and place my finger into the mark of the nails, and place my hand into his side, I will never believe." [26] Eight days later, his disciples were inside again, and Thomas was with them. Although the doors were locked, Jesus came and stood among them and said, "Peace be with you." [27] Then he said to Thomas, "Put your finger here, and see my hands; and put out your hand, and place it in my side. Do not disbelieve, but believe." [28] Thomas answered him, "My Lord and my God!" [29] Jesus said to him, "Have you believed because you have seen me? Blessed are those who have not seen and yet have believed" (John 20:24-28, NLT).

"These wounds (from the spear and the nails) are real, Thomas. Put your fingers into them to see that I am not just a spirit." That is a paraphrase of what Jesus said to Thomas. Thomas didn't doubt, he wanted solid proof. So, Jesus gave it to Him.

"For our sake he was crucified under Pontius Pilate; he suffered death and was buried. On the third day he rose again in accordance with the Scriptures; he ascended into Heaven and is seated at the right hand of the Father. He will come again in glory to judge the living and the dead, and his kingdom will have no end." – Nicene Creed (partial)

Chapter Eight

NOT WHAT BUT WHO IS THE TRINITY?

The Godhead/Trinity/Triune God

The Trinity is the most commonly used term for God the Father, the Son, and the Holy Spirit. Some groups use the term "Godhead" and others refer to the "Triune" God. The term used does not matter as long as the user is trying to describe our extremely unique Creator. Is Christianity polytheistic (many gods) or monotheistic (one god)? People who like to argue over such things say it is monotheistic and definitely NOT polytheistic. Critics in related religions claim we are practicing polytheism. Everybody wants to win the argument. I am just a layperson, but I've walked this Walk and read, studied, and taught it's precepts for almost 4 decades; and, you know what? I don't think we can call Christianity either one of them! It is unique! God is unique! There are not three distinct "gods" but neither is there an entity that can only operate as one "being" at a time. The balance in this is found in the reading and study of the Word (in context, not singling out "bullet" scriptures), in prayer, and in developing your personal relationship with the God of the Word!

The "Jesus Only" Argument

There are those who claim there is no Trinity or Godhead and that God is only one being. They say that when Jesus was on Earth, God was only on Earth. When He went to Heaven, all of God was back in Heaven. Among other names, this is called the "Jesus only" belief system. They, and others, say that God is only one entity (actually He is) and not three (actually He is) simply because it is inconceivable in human reasoning. (And they have ignored a lot of scripture, some of which will be quoted in this chapter.) *God ain't human, folks! So, get over it.* It is not polytheism in the idea of multiple gods. It is not "monotheism" as most think of it. God is the Ultimate multi-tasker and has the attributes to do it all at one time. He can manifest in more than one place at a time performing multiple functions while still balancing the universe in His other hand! We simply cannot conceive of that from a human standpoint. *So, let's quit trying to figure out God and just believe Him for once!*

Somehow beyond our reasoning power, God is three Entities wrapped up into One! The inspired author of the book of Genesis (Moses is considered to be the author) wrote this narrative, "[26] Then God said, "Let *us* make human beings in *our image, to be like us* [my italics]. They will reign over the fish in the sea, the birds in the sky, the livestock, all the wild animals on the earth, and the small animals that scurry along the ground" (Genesis 1:26, NLT).

Even as secular a person as Sigmund Freud picked up on one aspect in our reflection of God's image many years ago from a psychology standpoint. He observed that the human nature consisted of an id, an ego, and a superego. The id is the flesh desiring immediate gratification. The flesh, of course, does all the physical work and aids in many of the mental endeavors. The ego is the equivalent of the soul or mentality which is supposed to direct the flesh (id), but often falls prey to the same desires. It also does a lot of the day-to-day direction of projects, reasoning things out, planning, etc. The superego is the equivalent of the human spirit and, as psychology says it, when the superego (the human spirit in non-believers) is in supremacy, everything is in the proper order. The "superego" or human spirit (or conscience) is supposed to be the "overseer" and director of all functions. But, as Freud implied, this "overseeing" is a difficult proposition. [xvii]

So, in essence, we are a three-part being–spirit, soul, and flesh. Take any one of those away and we would not be "human." We could be a "ghost" (spirit only with a consciousness), a zombie (no soul), or a completely amoral depraved being – a socio/psychopath (no conscience). Likewise, God without His different attributes/personalities would not be the God of the Word, the God that created us.

The body, soul, and spirit of an un-saved person struggle for supremacy with the body and soul usually teaming up against the spirit. The human spirit, which was designed to be in control (prior to sin's inception in the Garden of Eden), is struggling for supremacy over the now voracious appetites of the body and soul. It normally loses. There are many people who are good people because as Freud would say–they have the super-ego in charge. They are "in control," but having to do it under their own fragile resolve. Therefore, hypertension, high blood pressure, depression, and mental disease and other disorders resulting from this struggle plague mankind. So, without any other options, there lay the human condition. A much superior option came when Jesus came along to offer us His help through the Holy Spirit to be our Guide, Comforter, and Counselor if we accept Him as our Lord and Saviour.

The author of Genesis goes on to say, "[27] So God created human beings *in his own image* [my italics]. In the image of God he created them; male and female he created them" (Genesis 1:27, NLT). So, we see that God made two entirely different genders *in (from) His image*. Even modern experts on the brain and reasoning will, despite political correctness, state that men's and women's brains are physiologically and psychologically different. They not only think differently, but communicate differently because of chemicals and other variances between male and female brains and, also, how they coordinate the use of the left and right sides of their brains. In a marriage relationship, these differing attributes should come together and complement each other rather than serve as a conflict.

I believe that this is another aspect of the scriptural reference where Jesus says that a married couple become one (person) instead of two, [4]"Haven't you read the Scriptures?" Jesus replied. "They record that from the beginning 'God made them male and female.'" [5]And he said, "This explains why a man leaves his father and mother and is joined to his wife, and the two are united into one.' [6]Since they are no longer two but one, let no one split apart what God has joined together" (Matthew 19:4-6, NLT).

The NIV, KJV, and some others also use the term "one flesh" to denote becoming one person. Eve was created from part of Adam's body according to Genesis. Before that, Adam was created in *His Image* (referring to the Godhead). *Did Adam therefore have all of God's mental/spiritual attributes which were then distributed between man and woman upon Eve's creation?* If that be true, then in a marriage these attributes are brought back together into one re-completed spiritual "entity or person."

(In general, one or the other gender is better than the other in various areas such as math or communication skills. There is a wealth of information at your library or, more current and quicker, on the web: WebMD (www.webmd.com); Brain Fitness for Life (www.brainfitnetnessforlife.com), and many others (just Google "differences in men's and women's brains").

Some people claim that God was talking to the angels in Genesis 1:26 when He said, "in our image" and "us." There are two problems with this thinking: 1) Angels are not creative beings so they were not involved in making man and women in their image! They are created beings. 2) It says that God created human beings in His own image, not any other entity's image. So, that puts the "our image" in verse 26 into "his own image" and "In the image of God…" in verse 27. There is also a third reason of sorts. If a person reads the entire Bible, in context with all its parts, he or she cannot, in good conscience, be able to not notice that God is not "singular." *He is something we cannot comprehend.* He is the One and yet He is the Three. He contains (since we are made in His image) all the attributes that "He" spread between the man and the woman.

The Son of God–Jesus

Most people understand that "Christianity" is named after Jesus Christ, the founder, in a manner of speaking. But Jesus Christ was not his name. Jesus is the English version of *Iesous* which is considered the Greek form for Yeshua (Joshua in English). Yeshua is the name derived from the Hebrew word for "to deliver" or "to rescue" – *a very appropriate name for the Eternal mission of this God-man called Jesus.*

Christ was not his surname. It is the English word for the Greek *Christós* which means "anointed." It also means, in English, "messiah," but this is, again, a title that just refers back to the term "anointed." So, what does anointed mean? Well, when you spread butter on a piece of toast that is sort of "anointing" the toast. You say, "What a heretical way to describe Jesus–a piece of toast!" Hang on; this is just a means of getting across the idea of anointing. When the butter melts into the toast, it permeates it, it flavors it. It is no longer just dry unappetizing toast; it has flavor now that "lactose tolerant" people can enjoy.

Now, Who is this Jesus Fellow Again?

Jesus, without the anointing of God, would just be a man. Well, I take that back — not quite. He did not have a human father. Having been a high school science teacher and taught biology and genetics, I can tell you that this is genetically and biologically impossible; humanly impossible. But nothing is impossible with God. (Some animals can produce offspring without a father, but all the offspring are female. This is called parthenogenesis.) Jesus once said to His disciples when discussing the salvation of the rich, [26]Jesus looked at them and said, "With man this is impossible, but with God all things are possible" (Matthew 19:26, NIV).

Now, what about Jesus? Some would say He is just a glorified man, born of God, but that is all. What if you saw that Jesus was part of God before the

115

creation of the world? That kind of destroys that argument. In the first letter to the Corinthian and Colossians churches, Paul said this:

> [6] But we know that there is only one God, the Father, who created everything, and we live for him. And there is only one Lord, Jesus Christ, through whom God made everything and through whom we have been given life. (1 Corinthians 8:6, NLT).
> [15] Christ is the visible image of the invisible God. He existed before anything was created and is supreme over all creation, [16] for through him God created everything in the heavenly realms and on earth. He made the things we can see and the things we can't see—such as thrones, kingdoms, rulers, and authorities in the unseen world. Everything was created through him and for him (Colossians 1:15-16, NLT).

Theologians argue over who wrote the book of Hebrews. Personally, I believe it was Paul, but no one is really sure. It seems to me the author uses the same thought processes. So, Paul (or whoever) in writing the Hebrews said, "[2] But now at last, God sent his Son to bring his message to us. God created the universe by His Son, and everything will someday belong to the Son" (Hebrews 1:2, CEV).

Jesus, the "Trouble-Maker"

Jesus did not sin, but He was well-known for stirring up the proverbial "hornet's nest" by discrediting some of the hundreds of man-made rules the scribes and religious leaders had burdened the people with over the centuries in addition to the Law of Moses. (It is not a sin to break a sin that is not a sin!) In fact, one author, Bruxy Cavey, points out that His first "joust" with all the religious clap-trap was at the wedding in Cana. In describing when Jesus turned approximately 120 gallons of water into high-quality wine for the wedding guests, he says:

116

Through his first miracle, Jesus intentionally desecrates a religious icon. He purposely chooses these sacred jars to challenge the religious system by converting them from icons of personal purification into symbols of relational celebration. Jesus takes us from holy water to wedding wine. From legalism to life. From religion to relationship.[xviii]

He went on to healing people on the Sabbath, pulling off heads of wheat and eating them on the Sabbath (work!), and other things to rub the religious authorities noses in their own legalism. *Jesus represents love, the religious authorities represented control.* I made the statement in a previous chapter that "Complexity leads to legalism, but simplicity (balance) leads to Jesus." Although we have difficulty understanding the concept of a God-man who dies for us and comes back from being very dead to be a Glorified Man, Jesus as a teacher kept things pretty simple. His stories were in simple terms and relevant concepts to the common people of the time. He took time to explain things to His disciples and inner circle in simple terms.

But that isn't the way the church world wants to present Him. His Church should be simple, but for many, the more elaborate the better. A. W. Tozer, among the other trends he noted in the church after WWII was the loss of "simplicity." This is what he said, "Every age has its own characteristics. Right now we are in an age of religious complexity. The simplicity which is in Christ is rarely found among us. In its stead are programs, methods, organizations and a world of nervous activities which occupy time and attention but can never satisfy the longing of the heart. The shallowness of our inner experience, the hollowness of our worship, and that servile imitation of the world which marks our promotional methods all testify that we, in this day, know God only imperfectly, and the peace of God scarcely at all."[xix] Sounds a lot like today.

Back to "Jesus Only"

So how are God the Father and Jesus related? Are they one and the same? Is Jesus a "chip off the old block" (a real Son) or is He just a "good" man with a relationship with God? This is what Jesus said to His disciples one day, [27] "My Father has handed all things over to me. No one knows the Son except the Father. And nobody knows the Father except the Son and anyone to whom the Son wants to reveal him" (Matthew 11:27, CEB). It sounds like a pretty close relationship to me. If they are one and the same, why did the Father have to hand over authority to Jesus (if He is He)? And if they are not a close knit working relationship then why can only Jesus introduce people to the Father?

That was only one of many times that Jesus made similar comments to His followers; here is what Jesus said when the mother of James and John asked Jesus to let her boys sit on His left and right when He came into His kingdom: [23] Jesus told them, "You will indeed drink from my bitter cup. But I have no right to say who will sit on my right or my left. My Father has prepared those places for the ones he has chosen" (Matthew 20:23, NLT). Leave it to moms to look out for their sons' interests, but, actually these "saintly" apostles were frequently (prior to the crucifixion) jostling for a higher place in the "pecking order." (Read the Gospels!) So if Jesus and the Father are the same identical entity, why can't Jesus make that decision? Why also would He tell His disciples that only the Father knew the time of His return to judge the world, [36] "However, no one knows the day or hour when these things will happen, not even the angels in Heaven or the Son himself. Only the Father knows" (Matthew 24:36, NLT). Once again, if He is the Father, why doesn't He know? One last one–His prayer in the Garden of Gethsemane:

Jesus Prays in Gethsemane

> [36] Then Jesus went with them to the olive grove called Gethsemane, and he said, "Sit here while I go over there to pray." [37] He took Peter and Zebedee's two sons, James and John, and he became anguished and distressed. [38] He told them, "My soul is crushed with

grief to the point of death. Stay here and keep watch with me." [39] He went on a little farther and bowed with his face to the ground, praying, "My Father! If it is possible, let this cup of suffering be taken away from me. Yet I want your will to be done, not mine" (Matthew 26:36-39, NLT).

This scene in the garden shows the humanity of Jesus. He knew He was about to be beaten, whipped to a bloody mess, and then crucified shortly. (The word excruciating comes from the Latin for "crucifixion.") He was scared. "Oh! Heresy!" Some will proclaim! No, Jesus suffered and was tempted as a man. We read that scripture–remember? Would you not be afraid? I would be terrified, except, just as Jesus did when He prayed to the Father, I believe peace and comfort from the Father would come. Now to the point–if He and He are the same He, why would He be praying to Him (the Father)? We either have a Godhead which we cannot really comprehend and therefore come up with all kinds of human reasoning ideas, or Jesus, the Holy Spirit, and God the Father are the "One, but Three."

By the way, have you noticed that mankind's fall started in a garden (the first physical man) and, basically, ended (for those who follow God) in a garden where Jesus (the second and first Heavenly man) was arrested to be executed?

[46] What comes first is the natural body, then the spiritual body comes later. [47] Adam, the first man, was made from the dust of the earth, while Christ, the second man, came from heaven. [48] Earthly people are like the earthly man, and heavenly people are like the heavenly man (1 Corinthians 15:46-48, NLT).

Messiah–What is that?

I spoke earlier of the time God tested Abraham for his loyalty by telling him to sacrifice his "promised" son, Isaac, on Mt. Moriah. How God, at the last second, forbids him to kill his son and provides a ram for the sacrifice. As stated before, this was the first "substitutionary" sacrifice for a person. Of course, later the Mosaic Law set up substitutionary sacrifices, blood sacrifices, for the Israelites' sins. Now, came Jesus, the promised Son, the promised Messiah to permanently take away the sin of those who call on His name for salvation.

From the scriptures already read, we know that in order to make God the Father accessible to humans again, it required that: 1) Jesus, part of the Godhead, had to be tempted and suffer from that in order to be our "High Priest." A high priest who doesn't understand what it is like to be the person he is representing is not much of a high priest. The author of Hebrews said it this way, "[17] Therefore, he had to be made like his brothers and sisters in every way. This was so that he could become a merciful and faithful high priest in things relating to God, in order to wipe away the sins of the people" (Hebrews 2:17, CEB). How could a high priest who didn't understand the oppression of human sin, atone to Father God for it? 2) He had to be the Ultimate and Final blood sacrifice that permanently paid for our sins:

> [24] For Christ did not enter into a holy place made with human hands, which was only a copy of the true one in Heaven. He entered into heaven itself to appear now before God on our behalf. [25] And he did not enter heaven to offer himself again and again, like the high priest here on earth who enters the Most Holy Place year after year with the blood of an animal. [26] If that had been necessary, Christ would have had to die again and again, ever since the world began. But now, once for all time, he has appeared at the end of the age to remove sin by his own death as a sacrifice (Hebrews 9:24-26, NLT).

So there is Jesus Christ, our Savior, High Priest, Advocate, Counselor, Friend and Comforter. He paid an extremely high price to become those things and others to us; but primarily, He is our Savior which means when we call on Him to be our Friend and Master, we are separated from the world and, if we listen to our Savior (through the Holy Spirit) we will be different than we were before. This is what Peter said, "³ You have had enough in the past of the evil things that godless people enjoy—their immorality and lust, their feasting and drunkenness and wild parties, and their terrible worship of idols. ⁴ Of course, your former friends are surprised when you no longer plunge into the flood of wild and destructive things they do. So they slander you. ⁵ But remember that they will have to face God, who will judge everyone, both the living and the dead" (1 Peter 4:3-5, NLT).

God the Holy Spirit

Throughout the Bible there are references to the plurality of God. We have a body, a soul, and a spirit. God is a complex being. He is God the Father, God the Son, and God the Holy Spirit and each facet has a function. The Holy Spirit appears to be the Implementer. In chemistry, the term would be *catalyst*. A catalyst is a substance that causes or accelerates a chemical reaction without itself being affected.[xx] This is just by its presence. In human social terms, we could use the term *enabler*. Dictionary.com defines it this way: to make able; give power, means, competence, or ability to; authorize...." That is a much better idea of what the Holy Spirit does both in creative ability and what He does for the Christian believer.

In Genesis 1:1-3, the author shows an image of the Holy Spirit in this capacity, "¹ In the beginning God created the heavens and the earth. ² The earth was formless and empty, and darkness covered the deep waters. And the Spirit of God was hovering over the surface of the waters. ³ Then God said, "Let there be light," and there was light" (Genesis 1:1-3, NLT).

When Jesus was preparing to leave His disciples for Heaven (after His resurrection), He made a number of interesting statements regarding the Holy Spirit that show Him in the light of an enabler. According to the Apostle John's account, Jesus said to His disciples and apostles, "⁶ Rather, you are filled with grief because I have said these things. ⁷ But very truly I tell you, it is for your good that I am going away. Unless I go away, the Advocate will not come to you; but if I go, I will send him to you. [8] When he comes, he will prove the world to be in the wrong about sin and righteousness and judgment..." (John 16:6-8, NIV).

The Holy Spirit Inhabits Believers

Jesus says that the Holy Spirit—called the Advocate here—cannot come until He leaves (to be with the Father). He's going to His home in Heaven and the Holy Spirit is coming to inhabit His followers. A God that can only exist in one place at one time could not do this and would not be much more than an elevated "human" god like some religions that are confused with being Christian teach. The Apostle John related it this way, "When the Advocate comes, whom I will send to you from the Father—the Spirit of truth who goes out from the Father—he will testify about me" John 15:26 (NIV).

In his second letter to the Corinthian Church, Paul is telling the Thessalonians that it is not necessary to use big words or great speaking skills to teach them (or anyone) about God's Word (His plan). It is simply necessary to allow the Holy Spirit to aid the speaker (see 1 Cor. 2:1-8). He further says:

> [9] That is what the Scriptures mean when they say,
> "No eye has seen, no ear has heard,
> and no mind has imagined
> what God has prepared
> for those who love him."
> [10] But it was to us that God revealed these things by his Spirit. For his Spirit searches out everything and shows us God's deep secrets. [11] No one can know a person's thoughts except that person's own spirit, and no one can know God's thoughts except God's own Spirit. [12] And we have received God's Spirit (not the world's spirit), so we can know the wonderful things God has freely given us.

¹³ When we tell you these things, we do not use words that come
from human wisdom. Instead, we speak words given to us by the
Spirit, using the Spirit's words to explain spiritual truths. ¹⁴ But
people who aren't spiritual can't receive these truths from God's
Spirit. It all sounds foolish to them and they can't understand it,
for only those who are spiritual can understand what the Spirit
means (1 Corinthians 2:9-14, NLT).

Notice that in verse 11 it says that "no one can know a person's thoughts
except that person's own spirit, and no one can know God's thoughts except
God's own Spirit." We are made in the image of God. We have a spirit, but
until we accept Jesus as our Saviour, we do not have the Holy Spirit of God
instructing us. We only have our "spirit" which we commonly call our conscience
and Sigmund Freud called the "super-ego." This niche in our "mentality" called
the spirit becomes co-habited by the Holy Spirit when a person accepts Jesus
as his or her Saviour.

Jesus says, basically, that upon His arrival in Heaven, He will ask Father
God to send the Holy Spirit to His followers to testify (to them and others) about
Himself. Interestingly, several translations use the word "advocate" here which
basically means defense attorney. This is a term also used for Jesus position
between us (through the Holy Spirit) and God the Father. He acts as a "filter"
to remove our sinful nature before God the Father. The argument could be and
is presented by some that this doesn't mean that Jesus or the Holy Spirit are
partners in "God." Well, why is the Holy Spirit referred to in scripture as "God's
Holy Spirit" then? If you were to say that I had a bad spirit, you would still be
talking about me, not another entity.

The Apostle Matthew, in his gospel, said this, "This is how Jesus Christ was
born. A young woman named Mary was engaged to Joseph from King David's
family. But before they were married, she learned that she was going to have a
baby by God's Holy Spirit" (Matthew 1:18, CEV). Neither it nor any of the other
Gospels say God came down as one entity. There is one well-known religion

that believes that God (who to them is a glorified man who earned godhood and this planet) came down and had physical sex with Mary to impregnate her. This, like babies born in Heaven first (another of their beliefs), may have impregnated some people's understanding of what Christianity believes. It doesn't believe either one. Mary's pregnancy was a miracle as was foretold over centuries of prophecy (and babies aren't born to parents in Heaven first and then sent to Earth).

The Seal of Approval

The Holy Spirit in us is God's stamp of approval. With the Spirit's entry into your life, that "secret" hidden from the ancients comes true! Paul, writing to the Ephesians, stated, "[13] You too heard the word of truth in Christ, which is the good news of your salvation. You were sealed with the promised Holy Spirit because you believed in Christ. [14] The Holy Spirit is the down payment on our inheritance, which is applied toward our redemption as God's own people, resulting in the honor of God's glory" (Ephesians 1:13-14, CEB). Later, in the same letter, he said, "[30] And do not grieve the Holy Spirit of God, with whom you were sealed for the day of redemption" (Ephesians 4:30, NIV). In ancient times, many kings wore a special ring with their unique "seal" on it. On documents the king wrote, a patch of molten wax would be dripped on the edge of the document where it was sealed together. The king would press his seal (from the ring) into the wax to prove the document was from the king and no one else. God places His "seal" within us with a little "piece" of Himself.

The "Holy Spirit of God" is why our "image" of God has a spirit, a weak one, but a spirit. God's Spirit is hugely powerful and He uses it to do many things from causing Mary to become pregnant without any human input to the creation of the Earth. He uses the Holy Spirit to be our seal of God's approval and advisor. Notice in Ephesians 4 that we can still be crude and a lot of other bad things if we choose not to listen to the Holy Spirit's advice. His presence does not make us automatons. He is a Guide, Counselor, Advocate, Comforter and meets many other needs of the believer and He is both there with the believer and there with God the Father. He is never a dictator!

God lives within us in the Person of His Holy Spirit. This is BEYOND any type of earthly connection or relationship we can have with anyone or anything else! He does not force His Will upon us, but advises us if we continue to listen. Unlike human acquaintances, although He knows all of our secrets, He does not tell anyone about them. Paul told the Thessalonian Church, [16] "Rejoice always, [17] pray continually, [18] give thanks in all circumstances; for this is God's will for you in Christ Jesus. [19] Do not quench the Spirit" (1 Thessalonians 5:16-19, NIV). *Quench* means "to put out."

This is a DIRECT LINK to God through the Holy Spirit and Jesus. That ought to make us awe-struck just thinking about it, but most Christians just take it for granted. What do people do when they take something for granted? They don't take care of it, nurture it, water it or feed it and it withers and dies. No, God does not force His presence on us. We can "quench the Holy Spirit" as several translations of the Bible say it. Other words used are "stifle" and "suppress." The meaning is the same—we are the agent in cutting off communications with God, not Him! But if we seek Him and come close to Him, He will supply the Spirit in abundance!

John, in his gospel, said it this way, "[37] On the last day, the climax of the festival, Jesus stood and shouted to the crowds, "Anyone who is thirsty may come to me! [38] Anyone who believes in me may come and drink! For the Scriptures declare, 'Rivers of living water will flow from his heart.'" [39] [When he said "living water," he was speaking of the Spirit, who would be given to everyone believing in him. But the Spirit had not yet been given, because Jesus had not yet entered into his glory]" (John 7:37-39, NLT).

Back to the Trinity

From these verses, we see that, according to the authors of the Word (Bible) that as the Holy Spirit was the Enabler, Jesus was the Builder while God the

Father was the Architect in the Creation of everything we see and experience. God has a perfect plan and His different "facets" make it all possible. We need to be a lot, lot, lot more appreciative of His Love for us, His willingness to experience the suffering of temptation, the agony of torture and death (as a man called Jesus), and the fact that He could have just gotten totally fed up with mankind and wiped the Earth clean one more time and made a rock garden out of it! But He didn't. He loves His creation enough to plan millennia in advance for our mistakes and disobedience and set up a recovery system for us to come back to Him in grace.

The fact that you will, if seeking Him, know by experience that He really is there, is also the way God reassures us that He and this relationship are real. He is not some theological concept or a figment of our imagination. He is very, very real and will manifest Himself to you at the time, place and in the way that He deems best for you. Again, He is a personal God; personal down to the individual level. He knows you! (And you don't have to yell, scream, roll on the floor, etc. or follow a bunch of man-made rules and traditions to get His attention and love!) Those who deny and block off this connection out of fear, logic, or misperceptions due to having experienced bizarre religious behavior or religious legalism, miss the greatest benefit of being a Christian. Christianity is simple, it is balanced, and it is relationship, a personal relationship with the God of the cosmos!

Chapter Nine

WHAT ABOUT THE BIBLE–
WHAT IS IT?

—◦◦◦—

[5]Every word of God proves true.

He is a shield to all who come to him for protection.

[6]Do not add to his words,

or he may rebuke you and expose you as a liar

(Proverbs 30:5-6, NLT).

This proverb is not involved in policing the canon, because what we consider to be the Old Testament was not finished yet, and the New Testament lay centuries in the future. In fact, there is no statement in scripture about which books are canonical and which are not; the canon is determined by your church. The proverb warns us against a more fundamental, more serious sin: failing to distinguish between what God says and what we'd like Him to say, passing out our own opinions and traditions as if they were the very Word of God. Whether we do this by blatantly appending our own writings to the Bible and proclaiming it as God's Word or by more insidiously making our own interpretations into a new standard of orthodoxy, it is equally wrong[xxi] –Rev. Kenneth W. Collins

First a Note on Scripture Comprehension

The absolutely necessary way of comprehending concepts in the Bible is not just by reading and memorizing isolated scriptures, but by reading the entire Bible and taking everything in "context." (You can skip the genealogies if you wish, but later you might want to look at them in the context of a study of the birth of the Christ.) The complementary method is to ask the Holy Spirit to interpret it to you and to help you comprehend it. Scripture memorization can be helpful also, but one must keep it in perspective. Unfortunately, some people think memorizing "key" scriptures makes them an "expert" on the contents of the Bible and the intent of God. This person is often the co-worker who "shoots" you with a "scripture bullet" when (in their opinion) you have said something "heretical" (like "he sure is lucky!" or "God doesn't heal every time.") This type of behavior reflects very poorly on Christ. It comes off as condemning behavior, so if you are doing it–please stop!

Individual scriptures need to be kept in context, no matter how important they are, such as John 3:16, "[16] For God so loved the world, that he gave his only begotten Son, that whosoever believeth in him should not perish, but have everlasting life" (John 3:16, KJV). This is probably the most memorized scripture in the Bible. It is written beautifully in the King James and hasn't been changed much at all in any translation. It is part of a very important concept also–God's sacrificial love for mankind and Jesus as the key element of God's re-establishment of "personal" salvation (a personal "walk" with God). It is part of a greater message. Pray and work to be the person who knows the Bible and knows some memorized scriptures–the ones that inspire you; not as "scripture bullets" in your "Bible bandolier."

In context means that someone should not take a scripture, isolate it from the rest of the Bible, and build a new "idea or concept" which isn't in the original. Pastor Ken Collins addressed this in the beginning quote from his website. This can lead to a new church split, sect, denomination, or even a cult. Here are several warnings from the Bible about this tendency, several from Paul and one from Jesus:

[8] Let God's curse fall on anyone, including us or even an angel from heaven, who preaches a different kind of Good News than the one we preached to you (Galatians 1:8, NLT).

Warnings against False Teachers

4 Now the Holy Spirit tells us clearly that in the last times some will turn away from the true faith; they will follow deceptive spirits and teachings that come from demons. [2] These people are hypocrites and liars, and their consciences are dead. [3] They will say it is wrong to be married and wrong to eat certain foods. But God created those foods to be eaten with thanks by faithful people who know the truth (1 Timothy 4:1-3, NLT).

Warning about False Teachers

[3] If anyone teaches anything different and doesn't agree with sound teaching about our Lord Jesus Christ and teaching that is consistent with godliness, [4] that person is conceited. They don't understand anything but have a sick obsession with debates and arguments. This creates jealousy, conflict, verbal abuse, and evil suspicions (1 Timothy 6:3-4, CEB).

[18] And I solemnly declare to everyone who hears the words of prophecy written in this book: If anyone adds anything to what is written here, God will add to that person the plagues described in this book. [19] And if anyone removes any of the words from this book of prophecy, God will remove that person's share in the tree of life and in the holy city that are described in this book (Revelation 22:18-19, NLT).

It seems pretty obvious that God frowns upon adding to or subtracting from His Word, especially by people doing it intentionally to profit themselves. (Read Paul's letters and you will find this was a problem even in the first century church!) The warning Jesus gives in Revelation 22 is especially dire. Removal of that person's share from the "tree of life and in the holy city" appears to me to mean excommunication by God from His kingdom. Some people say this verse applies to the whole Bible. Maybe it does, but I'm kind of literal and it is talking about the prophecies in the Book of Revelation. The "Books" of the Bible were not put together as the Bible for several centuries after Revelation was written. I believe a person should be very, very careful if teaching on the book of Revelation to stick to the "book." A lot of the events in Revelation are obviously figurative so it leads to a desire to elaborate. As a once famous police detective, Joe Friday, on the old 50s and 60s television show, "Dragnet" always said, "Just the facts, ma'am, just the facts."

We need to keep to the facts of the Bible, but that can lead to the opposite problem, legalism, if you become too zealous of defending the "text." Speaking of text, many people have favorite translations and this is fine, as long as they don't claim that it is the only legitimate translation or only "authorized" translation. The *King James Version*, known in Colonial and prior times as *The Holy Bible*, has been abused in this way. It was written in beautiful ancient English prose (some experts say most of it came from the previously written Geneva Bible), but the Bible was originally written in Greek (common or *koine* Greek) and Hebrew. But between the "originals" and the King James and Geneva Bibles, it was written in Latin, the Latin Vulgate, for 1400 years. Greek and then Latin were the languages of the educated of The Holy Roman Empire and then early Europe.

I used the *King James Version* (KJV) early on in my walk (but had trouble understanding it), but my zeal for God came when, in my early 20s, I read the *The Living Bible* (TLB), a paraphrase not a translation. For once, I could comprehend what the Word said! From there I used the *New American Standard* (NASB), then the *New International Version* (NIV) and now for probably a decade the *New Living Translation* (NLT). Don't get me wrong, the King James (originally The Holy Bible) is an excellent translation and in some verses, more accurate in context, than some of the new translations; however, it is written in a dead language. We don't speak ancient British, nor do we comprehend it without training. A form of it is spoken on Pitcairn Island by the descendants of the HMS Bounty mutineers.

Today, with the electronic devices we have, a person can have nearly instant access to literally every know translation in virtually every primary language. When you get serious about the Word of God, it is wonderful to have various good translations at your fingertips. This is a time of transition, however. A story told recently by a local pastor about another pastor friend relates to the times. It seems that as that pastor was preaching down on the floor of the sanctuary of the church, as he paced back and forth in front of the congregation, he kept passing a fellow on the front row "playing" with his cell phone. Finally, he became so upset about this rude behavior that he snatched the phone from the man's hand and continued his sermon. After service, he found that the man was following the preacher's scriptures on his "smart" cell phone!

I believe that it is a sad statement on contemporary times in churches when you see numerous congregation members who bring no Bible to church with them. Now, if they have a good cell phone, iPad, or Notebook, they are without excuse.

A (Very) Brief History of the Bible

In a manner of speaking, the Bible goes back to Creation for the Bible is the history of mankind and the God Who created them and God's efforts to relate to this unique creature He had made "in His image." The Old Testament actual dates are indeterminate, but Moses is considered to be the author of the first 6 books: Genesis through Deuteronomy completing them around 1500 years before Christ. The rest of the 39 books of the Old Testament were written by leaders like Joshua, prophets, uncles (Esther's Uncle Mordecai), and kings (David and his son Solomon). The books of 1 and 2 Kings and 1 and 2 Chronicles which chronicle the kings and major events of first Israel and then the divided kingdoms of Judah and Israel were written by the prophets Jeremiah and Ezra respectively.

The Bible is a collection of documents from God-inspired authors through which the same vein runs–the fulfillment of prophecy in Jesus the Messiah and the establishment of the New Covenant Church. Testament and Covenant are used interchangeably, but New Covenant would be more accurate a description.

Testament infers written document such as a will. Its Latin origin basically meaning "to bear witness." It has also come to be expected terminology for the two major sections of the Bible–the Old (Covenant) Testament and the New (Covenant) Testament.

There is an approximate 400 year gap between what are considered to be "inspired" books of the Old Testament and the New Testament when Jesus came on the scene, fulfilled the Old Covenant and instituted the New Covenant between man and God. The Old Testament is as mentioned before includes a history of the Old Covenant made between God and Abraham and the Law given through Moses to the Israelites. Between the Old and New is the Apocrypha. The Apocrypha consists of 19 books filling in the history of the Israelites in the 400 year gap just mentioned.

The Apocrypha was not considered in the early church to be "inspired" but was considered important from the historical viewpoint. The word means non-canonical. Despite this, all the churches–Catholic, protestant, and orthodox continued to leave the Apocrypha in the Bible. While researching the internet, I found a website with an excellent but simple explanation of the history of these books. With his permission, here is what Reverend Kenneth W. Collins writes:

What Is the Apocrypha?

> The exact content of the Writings [sic] portion of the Hebrew Bible hadn't been fixed even by the New Testament era. The Jews in Alexandria and the Greek-speaking Diaspora had more books in this section of their Bible than the Jews in Palestine had in theirs, so we refer to them as the Alexandrian canon and the Palestinian canon. The books in the Alexandrian canon that do not appear in the Palestinian canon are called the Apocrypha or the "deuterocanonical books." The term "apocrypha" implies that the books are not canonical, while deuterocanonical means that they are latecomers to the canon. I'm using the term "apocrypha" only because it is more familiar to my readers.

Who Uses the Apocrypha?

> The ancient church universally used the Septuagint, which
> included what we call the Apocrypha. If a person says, "Our
> church is just like the first-century church," then for that to be
> true, they'd have to use Bibles that include the Apocrypha.

> By the fifth century, Latin had supplanted Greek as the language
> of the people in the western Roman Empire, so the bishop of
> Rome commissioned St. Jerome to make a new Latin translation
> of the Scriptures, because the older Latin ones were not very
> good. Jerome went to Bethlehem to learn Hebrew, where he
> discovered that some of the books in the Septuagint were not in
> the Palestinian canon. He decided they should not be part of the
> Bible and refused to translate them. Since those books were in
> liturgical use, the Roman church supplemented his translation with
> an older translation of the missing books. The result is called the
> Vulgate, which became the official Bible of the Roman Catholic
> Church for over 1,000 years.[xxii]

So, although not considered as "inspired" these books were considered to
be part of the "Bible" by the "mainline" church of that era. Later, during the
Protestant Reformation, they were not removed but afforded a separate section
of the Bible and still considered important for church functions, but not doctrinal.
A paragraph later, Reverend Collins goes on:

> All churches, Protestant, Catholic, and Orthodox, used the
> Apocrypha at the time of the Protestant Reformation. Martin
> Luther, who had a doctorate in biblical studies and knew German,
> Latin, Greek, and Hebrew, felt they could be used as a worship
> resource, for edification and morals, and so far as doctrine is

concerned, to corroborate it, but not to formulate it. That is pretty much the same as the Jewish principle that later books are less inspired than earlier books. This means that the Apocrypha, though part of the Bible, is barely inspired at all. Martin Luther translated the entire Bible into German, and in doing so, started the convention of placing the Apocrypha in a separate section, apart from the Old Testament and New Testament. All of the original Protestants used the Apocrypha, though, like everyone else, not very much. Three committees of translators produced the King James Version: one for the Old Testament, one for the Apocrypha, and one for the New Testament.

Who took the Apocrypha out of the Bible?

It was originally against the law to print an English-language Bible in America, because the Crown held the copyright to the King James Version, but it did not license any printers in the American colonies. The American Revolution made the United States an [sic] separate country at a time when there were no international copyright treaties. After the Revolution, it was legal to print English-language Bibles in America.

American printers discovered that they could leave out the Apocrypha and sell the Bible for the same price, and no one would care because it wasn't used much. Some of the homegrown religious groups naïvely assumed that whatever was not in their Bible was not in the canon. Later, when Catholics became a significant segment of the population, a non-Catholic would say, "That's not in the Bible" to a Catholic, completely unaware that it was the printer who left it out. A Lutheran pastor told me that one of his parishioners was insistent that the Lutheran Church did not recognize the Apocrypha as canonical. The parishioner was astonished when he saw the church by-law that says it is. Catholics, Protestants, and Orthodox Christians use the Apocrypha and it is part of the Bible for them. Many independent churches and low-church denominations think it is a Catholic addition when it is really a printer's subtraction. In other words, printers removed the Apocrypha from the Bible, not any church.[xxiii]

And all these years, I thought that some ancient church conference had removed it; so much for assumptions! At the end of the Revolutionary War, there were some very hard feelings toward our former mistress–England. Horrible abuse of American prisoners of war on disease infested rotting prison ships, abuse of captured families of some of our Founders. Coffee replaced tea and many things British were cast out. Perhaps this was one reason, but probably the motive was simply a thinner, less bulky Bible that could be sold for the same price. I buy older Bibles at garage sales, yard sales, and used book places and some years ago began to notice that Bibles not produced in or for the American market contained the Apocrypha.

I have recently begun to read the books of the Apocrypha and they have a wonderful amount of history of the captivities and struggles of the Jewish nation as it came out of the Persian empire to re-establish Jerusalem and Israel only to be conquered by the Romans and the beginnings of that struggle which gives insight on some of the religious leaders attitudes when Jesus came. There is some really good context material in the Apocrypha.

The inspired parts of the Bible do not cover secular history that correlates to events and people in scripture. If they did, they wouldn't be "inspired" and it would take an entire shelf for your "Bible." But studying the Apocrypha and historical sources can give a student of scripture insights to understand the characters and events in the Word even better. For instance, ever wonder where Moses was prior to killing that Egyptian overseer when he was age 40? Secular history tells us that he was the commander of the Egyptian army that routed the Ethiopians (current historical name) from conquered parts of Egypt. After driving them out of Egypt, he conquered Ethiopia, married the Ethiopian king's daughter and was, basically, the ruler of Ethiopia for a number of years before returning to Egypt.

The conquering general, a member son of the royal court returns home. Very popular types like that usually become presidents or prime ministers–maybe pharaoh? A challenge to whoever was in charge when he returned? Did you ever really think about it? Why would a high-up member of the royal family of Egypt flee for his life for killing a slave overseer for abusing slaves? Ancient Egypt was not a law and order republic! That is why just a cursory reading of scripture is not as interesting as a deeper study. The Bible, the Old Testament in particular, is full of intrigues, scoundrels, and heroes. Some of the scoundrels even become the heroes–Jacob would be a good example. But I digress.

Some claim that there are references in the New Testament to things only covered in apocryphal books. This is based upon some statements that resemble similar statements or events in Apocryphal books, but there is no hard evidence for this and really, it is a moot point. The argument is over whether the books are inspired or not with those "references" in the New Testament purportedly validating inspired status. As always, these types of arguments do nothing for the "cause of Christ" except turn people off and turn the proponents away from "Christ and Him crucified"—the central focus of Christianity.

To requote Paul in his letter to Timothy, "They don't understand anything but have a sick obsession with debates and arguments. This creates jealousy, conflict, verbal abuse, and evil suspicions (1 Timothy 6:4, CEB). Having a "sick obsession with debates and arguments" is something God had to cure me of many years ago. As my dad once said, "Son, you'd argue with a fence post!" It is not a good trait. We need to be ready to defend the Word of God and our commitment to the Christ, but not arguments that only hurt the hearer and our own walk with Jesus.

From early on, historically, the books of the Apocrypha have not been considered by the mainline churches as "inspired" but useful enough to keep in the Bible (except in the USA). There is much information available "online" about the Apocrypha and why it was removed. Apparently, it wasn't just for profit (also in England), but anti-Catholic feelings among Protestant and Anglican publishers. Again, do not let these arguments and arguers distract you from the relationship issue with Christ. The Apocrypha was an integral part of the Greek "Old Testament" the Septuagint and is a great source of historical data, at the very least.

Old Testament vs. New Testament

What is our relationship to the Old Testament? We don't live under the Old Covenant anymore! As mentioned in a previous chapter, there are two "veins" in the Old Testament—God's Promise to Abraham fulfilled by the birth of the Messiah and the Law of Moses given at a much later date to give the Israelites a structure to live by to keep them "holy." Jesus fulfilled the Promise and both fulfilled and replaced the Law of Moses with His love and the indwelling of Himself through the Holy Spirit. Many of the principles of the Law are still good, but they are in our "hearts" now through the guidance of the Holy Spirit. Much of the Old Testament is still instructive and edifying. As Paul said to Timothy, his young protégée evangelist and minister, "[16] All scripture is given by inspiration of God, and is profitable for doctrine, for reproof, for correction, for instruction in righteousness: [17] That the man of God may be perfect, thoroughly furnished unto all good works" (2 Timothy 3:16-17, KJV). The only documents at that early date considered "scripture" was what we call now the Old Testament and the Apocrypha both previously contained in the Septuagint.

We, as devout Christians, do not live by "rules and regulations" written in stone or on paper, especially the added-on rules of men! We have the scripture "written" in our hearts. Paul was pointing this out when talking about his desire that his fellow Jews would accept Jesus as the Messiah and comprehend that righteousness no longer came from observing the Law of Moses. He said this:

10 Dear brothers and sisters, the longing of my heart and my
prayer to God is for the people of Israel to be saved. ²I know
what enthusiasm they have for God, but it is misdirected zeal.
³For they don't understand God's way of making people right
with himself. Refusing to accept God's way, they cling to their
own way of *getting right with God by trying to keep the law* [my
italics]. ⁴For *Christ has already accomplished the purpose for
which the law was given* [my italics]. As a result, all who believe
in him are made right with God (Romans 10:1-4, NLT).

Peter himself, the recognized leader of the Jerusalem Church, noted that
even the devout couldn't keep the Law perfectly. When "Christians" within the
Jerusalem Church who had not yet given up their Pharisaical laws and rules
demanded that new Gentile Christians be circumcised and taught to follow the
Law of Moses, this how Peter responded:

> ⁴When they came to Jerusalem, they were welcomed by the church
> and the apostles and elders, to whom they reported everything God
> had done through them.⁵Then some of the believers who belonged
> to the party of the Pharisees stood up and said, "The Gentiles must
> be circumcised and required to keep the law [sic] of Moses."⁶
> The apostles and elders met to consider this question. ⁷After
> much discussion, Peter got up and addressed them: "Brothers,
> you know that some time ago God made a choice among you
> that the Gentiles might hear from my lips the message of the
> gospel and believe. ⁸God, who knows the heart, showed that he
> accepted them by giving the Holy Spirit to them, just as he did to
> us. ⁹He did not discriminate between us and them, for he purified
> their hearts by faith. ¹⁰Now then, why do you try to test God by
> putting on the necks of Gentiles a yoke that neither we nor our
> ancestors have been able to bear? ¹¹No! We believe it is through

the grace of our Lord Jesus that we are saved, just as they are (Acts 15:4-11, NIV).

What Peter was saying was that even the legal experts and Pharisees were not able to keep all of the strictures of the Law of Moses, much of the reason being that they had added even more rules, especially about how to keep the Sabbath. In fact, in trying so hard to fulfill all the requirements, they lost sight of the whole intent of the Law. They had to become hypocrites, as Jesus referred to them often, to look like they were perfectly following the Law. This is what Jesus said to the legal experts and Pharisees one day, "[22] And when you swear 'by heaven,' you are swearing by the throne of God and by God, who sits on the throne. [23] "What sorrow awaits you teachers of religious law and you Pharisees. Hypocrites! For you are careful to tithe even the tiniest income from your herb gardens, but you ignore the more important aspects of the law—justice, mercy, and faith. You should tithe, yes, but do not neglect the more important things. [24] Blind guides! You strain your water so you won't accidentally swallow a gnat, but you swallow a camel!"[5] (Matthew 23:22-24, NLT)

I have always enjoyed reading verse 24. It reminds me of a more modern expression–"Swatting at mosquitos while elephants stampede through the camp!" Obsession with detail and loss of perspective of the whole picture is what happens when you base things on a set of rules. The "categorizers" take over. They love rules. It makes them feel comfortable, the more rules they add. Actually, there is nothing wrong with rules as long as they are kept simple and few in number. All God told Moses was, "[8] Remember the Sabbath day, to keep it holy (Exodus 20:8, KJV). Beyond that, He said do this because He had set the example by creating everything in 6 days and resting on the seventh. The religious scribes and Pharisees had added an incredible number of "things" that constituted "work on the Sabbath."

---

5   Many English Bible translations picked up on "strain at gnats" (Matt. 23:2) centuries ago and kept repeating it. The original was not about getting eyestrain but about keeping bugs and sediment out of your drinking cup. Jesus used this idea of a ridiculously large object by using "camels" more than once.

Just for this Commandment, they wrote a book of things that were to be considered work called the Mishnah. This was expanded by commentaries explaining the rules in the Mishnah called the Gemora; both were included in the Torah. One simple principle became volume (or scroll) upon volume of how not to keep the Sabbath Day. They had lost focus on the purpose of the Sabbath. Many of them are simply ridiculous and some horrendous. Ridiculous–no one could write more than two alphabetic letters in any kind of permanent ink in one day, right-handed or left-handed! Horrendous—you could only *maintain* a person's injured or sick condition on the Sabbath. To add ointment or doing anything healing would violate the Sabbath! The rules became all that mattered; although, originally, they were intended to help people to behave, do their jobs and live their lives successfully. The "categorizers" just got out of control. And the religious experts, Pharisees and Sadducees took this stuff "deadly serious."

That is what Jesus, who as a partner in the Trinity originally established a much simpler law for the Israelites, had to contend with. That is why He habitually violated these "man-made laws." The Word says that Jesus was without sin (see Hebrews 4:14-16). If the laws He and His disciples were breaking (not washing hands, eating grain off the stalks of wheat on the Sabbath, healing on the Sabbath) were of God, then Jesus would have been sinning, but he wasn't because these were phony man-created religious strictures. The changeover from the Old Covenant to the New is described by Paul in this way:

> [16] And since Abraham and the other patriarchs were holy, their descendants will also be holy—just as the entire batch of dough is holy because the portion given as an offering is holy. For if the roots of the tree are holy, the branches will be, too. [17] But some of these branches from Abraham's tree—some of the people of Israel—have been broken off. And you Gentiles, who were branches from a wild olive tree, have been grafted in. So now you also receive the blessing God has promised Abraham and his children, sharing in the rich nourishment from the root of God's

special olive tree. [18] But you must not brag about being grafted in to replace the branches that were broken off. You are just a branch, not the root.

[19] "Well," you may say, "those branches were broken off to make room for me." [20] Yes, but remember—those branches were broken off because they didn't believe in Christ, and you are there because you do believe. So don't think highly of yourself, but fear what could happen. [21] For if God did not spare the original branches, he won't spare you either.

[22] Notice how God is both kind and severe. He is severe toward those who disobeyed, but kind to you if you continue to trust in his kindness. But if you stop trusting, you also will be cut off. [23] And if the people of Israel turn from their unbelief, they will be grafted in again, for God has the power to graft them back into the tree. [24] You, by nature, were a branch cut from a wild olive tree. So if God was willing to do something contrary to nature by grafting you into his cultivated tree, he will be far more eager to graft the original branches back into the tree where they belong (Romans 11:16-24, NLT).

In verse 17, Paul talks about how many Israelites "didn't make the cut." They refused to believe in the long awaited Messiah when He came. They removed themselves from the Abraham's olive tree. Gentiles had become Jews through proselytization before, but now the Hebrew nation, God's children, were no longer an exclusive club. Membership was now open to any non-Jewish person who accepted Jesus and became a member of the New Covenant Church and you did not have to become Jewish to join. Some of these gentile "Christians" over the centuries have treated Jewish people with disdain or worse. Crusaders slaughtered Jews (man, woman, and child) with the Muslims they encountered inside of Jerusalem when they conquered it (this isn't revisionist, politically corrected history). They seemed to forget that God came as a Jew, not gentile.

In verse 18, Paul was warning Gentiles who were now part of the family of God, not to get "cocky" about it and malign their Jewish brethren. In fact, in verse 23, he says that any future Jewish person who accepts Jesus will be grafted back in again. Their ancestors originally had the "right" to be part of this New Covenant Church of Jesus Christ. They still have the right to return and God is eager for them to return.

He hasn't rejected the Jewish nation. He made a promise to their ancestor Abraham that still stands. Some people seem to think that the Holocaust was God's judgment on them (or lack of divine protection) for rejecting His Son. This is not true. God sent prophets to the Jews living in Germany and Europe to warn the Jewish people to leave Europe entirely. Many took God's prophets seriously and left to the Americas and other safer places; most did not. Despite the fact that some persecution had already begun in Germany, only about 20 percent of German Jews left the country.

God is eager for them to return to the new sheepfold. He still loves them as any parent still loves a disobedient child, but can only pray for them and try to shield them from the consequences of their mistakes and bad decisions. So, we have Jesus Christ, but don't make the mistake of being arrogant and looking down on Jewish people. "For if God did not spare the original branches, he won't spare you either" (Romans 11:21, NLT).

Our Relationship to Judaism and the Old Testament

The whole history of the Old Testament and Judaism is the foundation upon which Christianity is built. Romans 10:4 (NIV) says that, "Christ is the culmination of the Law." Culmination means the intended results of the process. The *Common English Bible* (CEB) "cuts to the chase" by saying, "Christ is the goal of the Law, which leads to righteousness for all who have faith in God." This is why Paul, the Apostle, said that not a "jot or a tittle" of the Law has gone away, but that we are no longer under the Law. When one builds a house, the first thing the builder should do is build a solid, dependable foundation; but if the builder stopped with that, it wouldn't be a livable dwelling! The inhabitants would be constantly exposed to the elements. God didn't stop with the Law. It was a phase in His plan.

Jesus is that foundation. He replaced the old foundation of the Law of Moses since God was building His ultimate dream house for all mankind not just the Israelites. The Law would not support the new structure; it was a radically new design built to be durable enough to withstand different building concepts and builders. As Paul said, "[10] Because of God's grace to me, I have laid the foundation like an expert builder. Now others are building on it. But whoever is building on this foundation must be very careful. [11] For no one can lay any foundation other than the one we already have—Jesus Christ. [12] Anyone who builds on that foundation may use a variety of materials—gold, silver, jewels, wood, hay, or straw. [13] But on the judgment day, fire will reveal what kind of work each builder has done. The fire will show if a person's work has any value" (1 Corinthians 3:10-13, NLT).

The old foundation had to go. It supported the previous building as well as mankind allowed it to in their lives; but something far better would support the mansion that God had in mind. In Paul's second letter to the Corinthian Church, he covers this quite well:

The Glory of the New Covenant

> [7] The old way, with laws etched in stone, led to death, though it began with such glory that the people of Israel could not bear to look at Moses'[sic] face. For his face shone with the glory of God, even though the brightness was already fading away. [8] Shouldn't we expect far greater glory under the new way, now that the Holy Spirit is giving life? [9] If the old way, which brings condemnation, was glorious, how much more glorious is the new way, which makes us right with God! [10] In fact, that first glory was not glorious at all compared with the overwhelming glory of the new way. [11] *So if the old way, which has been replaced, was*

glorious, how much more glorious is the new, which remains forever [my italics]!

[12] Since this new way gives us such confidence, we can be very bold. [13] We are not like Moses, who put a veil over his face so the people of Israel would not see the glory, even though it was destined to fade away. [14] But the people's minds were hardened, and to this day whenever the old covenant is being read, the same veil covers their minds so they cannot understand the truth. And this veil can be removed only by believing in Christ. [15] Yes, even today when they read Moses'[sic] writings, their hearts are covered with that veil, and they do not understand.

[16] But whenever someone turns to the Lord, the veil is taken away. [17] *For the Lord is the Spirit, and wherever the Spirit of the Lord is, there is freedom* [my italics]. [18] So all of us who have had that veil removed can see and reflect the glory of the Lord. And the Lord—who is the Spirit—makes us more and more like him as we are changed into his glorious image (2 Corinthians 3:7-18, NLT).

Rules only bring condemnation, but as verse 17 says, "For the Lord is the Spirit, and wherever the Spirit of the Lord is, there is freedom." If Paul (who tried hard for a highly educated and brilliant man to communicate in "common" language) was trying to explain this concept to us "on the street" somewhere, maybe a coffeehouse and we weren't getting it, he might elaborate on it this way in more commonly understood terms:

Lifting the Veil

[7-8] The Government of Death, its constitution chiseled on stone tablets had a dazzling inaugural. Moses's face as he delivered the tablets was so bright that day (even though it would fade soon enough) that the people of Israel could no more look right at him than stare into the sun. How much more dazzling,

then, the Government of Living Spirit?[9-11] If the Government of Condemnation was impressive, how about this Government of Affirmation? Bright as that old government was, it would look downright dull alongside this new one. If that makeshift arrangement impressed us, *how much more this brightly shining government installed for eternity* [my italics]?

[12-15] With that kind of hope to excite us, nothing holds us back. Unlike Moses, we have nothing to hide. Everything is out in the open with us. He wore a veil so the children of Israel wouldn't notice that the glory was fading away—and they *didn't* notice. They didn't notice it then and they don't notice it now, *don't notice that there's nothing left behind that veil* [my italics]. Even today when the proclamations of that old, bankrupt government are read out, they can't see through it. Only Christ can get rid of the veil so they can see for themselves that there's nothing there.[16-18] *Whenever, though, they turn to face God as Moses did, God removes the veil and there they are—face-to-face! They suddenly recognize that God is a living, personal presence, not a piece of chiseled stone* [my italics] (2 Corinthians 3:7-18, MSG).

We are no longer under the Law engraved in stone! The "written" Law stood between a Holy God and man. That was the "veil" as Paul refers to it between man and the Glory of God.[6] That Glory in Moses's face was fading and Paul uses this to emphasize that from being established the Law was "fading" until the day the Messiah fulfilled it and it ceased to be our residence. We moved out of the crawlspace in the old foundation, dusted ourselves off and began to reside in the beautiful house God has given us! And He lives in it with us! He

---

6   When you read about Jesus crucifixion, notice that at the moment of His death, after He had cried out, "it is finished", the veil in the Temple that had separated mankind from the Holy of Holies portion of the temple was supernaturally ripped in two "from top to bottom." (The "Gospels" do not cover all the same facts, so read all accounts.) What a visual symbol to the Jewish nation that they could have direct access to God now without the need for a priest and a yearly sacrifice.

didn't reside in the crawlspace of the old "pier and beam" foundation. He only visited once in a while, but he stayed out in the yard (garden for you British folks) while talking to us through special persons–Moses, Joshua, judges and prophets. He didn't care to crawl around under the house with us. Time has no meaning to God; He was looking forward to the mansion which would go on top of that foundation where He would live with us!

An Explanation of Translation of Biblical Works

First off, the King James (the First) Version is NOT the first or only "authorized" English language version of the Bible. King Henry the 8th was actually the first monarch (government) to authorize the printing of an English Bible called *The Great Bible* in 1539.[xxiv] Queen Elizabeth I authorized the Geneva Bible, started in Geneva in 1557, but not published in England until 1575 with Elizabeth's blessing. There is some terrifically interesting history in the development of the Bible into people's contemporary languages, particularly English. That language translation was resisted to the point of burning people at the stake for attempting to deny state churches their "lockdown" on scripture knowledge. I won't even try to get into that here. There are a lot of really excellent sources on the web—just watch out for bias in some of them.

I have actually developed a much greater respect for the original King James translation while developing this book, but it is not in my "mother tongue." I couldn't understand it as a boy or young man. Please don't give only a KJV Bible to a new Christian in the 21st century. If you love the KJV and want the convert to enjoy it give it, but also give them a good translation written in contemporary language so they can read both and compare. It makes an incredible addition to a mature Christian's library, but expecting a new Christian to comprehend it immediately is like giving a famished person a difficult riddle to have to solve before they are allowed to eat.

There, I've said it and will get hate mail now from some individuals. There are actually some church congregations out there whose main doctrinal set-piece is not Jesus, but that the *King James Version* (original as they know it; the original had the Apocrypha and cross-references to it in it) is *the only allowable* translation for use by Christians. King James assembled a pretty diverse and knowledgeable translation team, but so had the writers of the Geneva Bible decades before and many other Bible publishers ever since. In the interim, more documents have been recovered. The Dead Sea scrolls are one incredible example, but others have been found, sometimes older translations overlooked in plain sight.

Most translation teams picked are from multiple denominations and scholarly fields within Christianity. When they get to the work of translation, they use the earliest, most reliable documents available. With electronic media, documents are a lot more available now than in the past. The art of translation has centuries of corporate knowledge and experience in translating ancient languages to draw upon today. One challenge was that Hebrew — after the destruction of Jerusalem and deportation of the Jews by the Romans — basically became a dead language that few knew.[7]

There is a spectrum of ways to do translation work from *formal equivalence* meaning basically "word for word, sentence structure for sentence structure" translation to *dynamic equivalence* which "means meaning to meaning to" or "effect on hearer/reader to effect on hearer/reader." Since many words in ancient Greek and Hebrew have no English equivalent word or may have been idiom (sayings) that make no sense today with their original cultural context, it is quite a challenge to translate a "new" Bible. Language changes constantly, despite the best efforts of all the dedicated English teachers of the land. This is another reason for the necessity of contemporary translations.

Formal equivalent translation, by nature, cannot be completely word-for-word. It would the same effect as if you were walking through an incredibly beautiful area, but are watching each carefully-placed footstep instead. Some

---

7   With the rebirth of Israel in 1948, Hebrew had to be "reinvented" so that a common and ancestrally accurate language would be the common language of the descendants of exiles coming from all over the world with a plethora of diverse tongues. It was no longer spoken and most Jews couldn't even read it.

word-for-word renditions would make absolutely no sense at all to the reader. Likewise, if you stretch dynamic equivalency too far, you are no longer translating but paraphrasing. "Functional equivalency" is a "spin-off" so to speak of dynamic. It deals with words that say one thing like "brothers" (used until recently to address the entire audience but especially in ancient times), but mean another thing. Depending upon whether it really seems to be addressing only males or a mixed audience, it will be rendered either "brothers" or "brothers and sisters." Let's remember, also, that the original documents were written in "common" Greek which would be like saying regular English is not formal high-English.

From my experience, translations using formal equivalency tend to be overly formal, with sometimes ponderous sentence structure, and with many meanings obscured by big words and formal language. Therein lays one major difference in interpretation by the reader. When reading a heavily formal equivalency translated document, one often has to do additional study to comprehend what it is saying whereas in dynamic or functional equivalency the meaning is (hopefully) readily apparent. A good example is the scene where Joseph and Mary take the baby Jesus to the Temple to dedicate their first born son to the Lord and they meet Simeon:

[22] And when the days of her purification according to the law of Moses were accomplished, they brought him to Jerusalem, to present him to the Lord; [23] (As it is written in the law of the Lord, Every male that openeth the womb shall be called holy to the Lord;) And to offer a sacrifice according to that which is said in the law of the Lord, a pair of turtledoves, or two young pigeons. [25] And, behold, there was a man in Jerusalem, whose name was Simeon; and the same man was just and devout, *waiting for the consolation of Israel* [my italics]: and the Holy Ghost was upon him. [26] And it was revealed unto him by the Holy Ghost, that he should not see death, before he had seen the Lord's Christ (Luke 2:22-26, KJV).

The New International Version uses the same terminology in verse 25 about "waiting for the consolation of Israel." The "And..." statement in 25 makes it sound like this verse is an "additional" event besides the "consolation of Israel." Both the NIV and KJV are about as much formal equivalency as possible with the *New International Version* actually being created by a team headed by a man who loved the King James, but found he could not use it with any success to approach contemporary American English speaking people about the Lord. The problem is that language has changed.

The consolation of Israel is the arrival of the Messiah. You can get this through context if you are practiced at using context, but consolation throws the modern person off. At least in the USA (a nation of competitors), it is associated with getting the "consolation" (booby/loser's) prize. I used the New American Standard and then the New International Version for decades and learned how to interpret them, but when I came across the functional equivalent-derived New Living Translation, I've used it ever since (while still comparing it to other good translations). It is really a personal choice what translation works for each person, based upon ability to comprehend concepts behind words or phrases, spiritual maturity, experience with studying and teaching the Word itself, and other nuances that are basically unexplainable. Pick the reliable translation that works for you as your primary Bible, the one that connects you with God.

Chapter Ten

WHAT IS AND ISN'T CHRISTIAN DOCTRINE?
(and Personal Conviction)

—————

I f there is one book (really one of Paul's letters) in the New Testament that
outlines proper church doctrine, it is Romans. Both of the Corinthian letters
have some very good direction in them; also, particularly on how spiritual gifts
are to be used properly in a church service. First however—what do we mean
by doctrine, an oft misused word.

> Doctrine: -ism, philosophical system, philosophy, school of
> thought—a belief (or system of beliefs) accepted as authoritative
> by some group or school.[xxv]
> CHURCH DOCTRINE (noun). The noun CHURCH DOCTRINE
> has 1 sense:
> **1.** the [sic] written body of teachings of a religious group that are
> generally accepted by that group.[xxvi]

Good examples of written and recited doctrines that state the core doctrines
of the Christian faith are "the Nicene Creed" and "Apostles' Creed." The Nicene
Creed, also known as "the Constantinopolitan Creed" (but no one can pronounce

it!) was written in AD 381 by the Council of Constantinople to deal with various heresies that were arising in the official church and creating problems. This is what it says:

Nicene Creed

We believe in one God,
the Father, the Almighty
maker of heaven and earth,
of all that is, seen and unseen.
We believe in one Lord, Jesus Christ,
the only Son of God,
eternally begotten of the Father,
God from God, Light from Light,
true God from true God,
begotten, not made,
of one Being with the Father.
Through him all things were made.
For us men and for our salvation
he came down from heaven:
by the power of the Holy Spirit
he became incarnate from the Virgin Mary, and was made man.
For our sake he was crucified under Pontius Pilate;
he suffered death and was buried.
On the third day he rose again
in accordance with the Scriptures;
he ascended into heaven
and is seated at the right hand of the Father.
He will come again in glory to judge the living and the dead,
and his kingdom will have no end.
We believe in the Holy Spirit, the Lord, the giver of Life,
who proceeds from the Father and the Son.

With the Father and the Son he is worshipped and glorified.

He has spoken through the Prophets.

We believe in one holy catholic and apostolic Church.

We acknowledge one baptism for the forgiveness of sins.

We look for the resurrection of the dead,

and the life of the world to come. Amen.

It contains the "facts." These are the basic truths of Christianity which no one involved in the inception of the Christian faith during the first few centuries could dispute. Anything added above these statements drifts into sectarianism or even cultism. The Nicene Creed is accepted by most denominations and recited in many mainline churches (to remind members what is doctrinal). The Apostles Creed just came about through common usage somewhere in the early centuries of the church. It is much shorter and simpler than the Nicene Creed, but still contains the essentials. This one is sometimes slightly altered by different denominations. The one quoted here is the universal version compiled by the English Language Liturgical Consultation (ELLC):

The Apostles' Creed

I believe in God, the Father almighty,

creator of heaven and earth.

I believe in Jesus Christ, God's only Son, our Lord,

who was conceived by the Holy Spirit,

born of the Virgin Mary,

suffered under Pontius Pilate,

was crucified, died, and was buried;

he descended to the dead.

On the third day he rose again;

he ascended into heaven,

he is seated at the right hand of the Father,

and he will come to judge the living and the dead.
I believe in the Holy Spirit,
the holy catholic Church,
the communion of saints,
the forgiveness of sins,
the resurrection of the body,
and the life everlasting. Amen.

Note that the Apostle's Creed is a shorter, more succinct parallel of the Nicene Creed. It still contains all the "nuggets" (I'm referring to gold not chicken) of the Christian Faith. These two creeds, each, contain the essential doctrinal beliefs of a Christian. There are other things that some groups try to pass off as necessary doctrines which are really just "personal convictions" of the group or founder(s) of the group. Notice that in the Nicene Creed it refers to the Holy Spirit as "He" not "It." In both creeds, the word "catholic" does not mean the Catholic Church. Catholic means universal in extent–the universal church.

Personal Conviction

I talked a little about this in the chapter on "Trials, Temptations, and Sin" when discussing whether a person that enjoys oysters on the half-shell should not eat that around someone who has a "religious" conviction about it. (But they could if the person just doesn't want to eat them themself.) That is personal conviction and something "convicted" Christians often try to enforce as "doctrine" on others or condemn other Christians for doing. Let's take a look at what the Apostle Paul in the 14th chapter of Romans had to say about this issue. Suffice to say that if you belong to or join a group that espouses a personal conviction as a doctrinal sin, you are held to it because you have accepted it doctrinally by joining their fellowship. If you know it is a only personal conviction that you do not want to apply to your life, you need to move to a congregation that is in agreement with what you know or to one that understands the concept of personal conviction as the Apostle Paul describes it. Let's see what Paul says:

The Danger of Criticism

14 Accept other believers who are weak in faith, and don't argue with them about what they think is right or wrong. [2] For instance, one person believes it's all right to eat anything. But another believer with a sensitive conscience will eat only vegetables. [3] *Those who feel free to eat anything must not look down on those who don't. And those who don't eat certain foods must not condemn those who do, for God has accepted them.* [4] *Who are you to condemn someone else's servants? Their own master will judge whether they stand or fall* [my italics]. And with the Lord's help, they will stand and receive his approval. [5] In the same way, some think one day is more holy than another day, while others think every day is alike. You should each be fully convinced that whichever day you choose is acceptable. [6] *Those who worship the Lord on a special day do it to honor him. Those who eat any kind of food do so to honor the Lord, since they give thanks to God before eating. And those who refuse to eat certain foods also want to please the Lord and give thanks to God.* [7] *For we don't live for ourselves or die for ourselves.* [8] *If we live, it's to honor the Lord. And if we die, it's to honor the Lord* [my italics]. So whether we live or die, we belong to the Lord. [9] Christ died and rose again for this very purpose—to be Lord both of the living and of the dead. [10] So why do you condemn another believer? Why do you look down on another believer? Remember, we will all stand before the judgment seat of God. [11] For the Scriptures say, "'As surely as I live,' says the Lord, 'every knee will bend to me, and every tongue will confess and give praise to God.'" [12] Yes, each of us will give a personal account to God. [13] So let's stop condemning

each other. Decide instead to live in such a way that you will not cause another believer to stumble and fall.

[14] I know and am convinced on the authority of the Lord Jesus that no food, in and of itself, is wrong to eat. But if someone believes it is wrong, then for that person it is wrong [my italics]. *[15]* And if another believer is distressed by what you eat, you are not acting in love if you eat it. Don't let your eating ruin someone for whom Christ died. *[16]* Then you will not be criticized for doing something you believe is good. *[17] For the Kingdom of God is not a matter of what we eat or drink, but of living a life of goodness and peace and joy in the Holy Spirit* [my italics]. *[18]* If you serve Christ with this attitude, you will please God, and others will approve of you, too. *[19]* So then, let us aim for harmony in the church and try to build each other up. *[20]* Don't tear apart the work of God over what you eat. Remember, all foods are acceptable, but it is wrong to eat something if it makes another person stumble. *[21]* It is better not to eat meat or drink wine or do anything else if it might cause another believer to stumble. *[22] You may believe there's nothing wrong with what you are doing, but keep it between yourself and God. Blessed are those who don't feel guilty for doing something they have decided is right. [23] But if you have doubts about whether or not you should eat something, you are sinning if you go ahead and do it. For you are not following your convictions. If you do anything you believe is not right, you are sinning* [my italics] (Romans 14, NLT).

The implication in verse 14:1 is that "weaker" Christians will usually be more restrictive on themselves. Their faith is not mature so they may have reservations about certain foods, etc. that a more mature or knowledgeable Christian knows are okay. They may also just have dietary reservations about

155

eating meat or other items of food. They may have a weakness or bad memories in that area because of misuse/abuse by a family member or themselves at one time. In either case, it is a sin for them to eat such things as they will violate their level of faith/conviction.

Verse three is very important guidance in this area of personal conviction. It is not good, that if you know someone believes it is sinful to eat or drink something to do it intentionally in their presence. It is equally wrong for them, if they see you somewhere else eating or drinking something they disapprove of to criticize you. God sees us, saves us, and gives us faith and grace as individuals, not as a group. This is another reason not to call Christianity a religion! In religions (including the "Christian religion" not Christianity), one set of very restrictive rules applies to everyone. There are some basic "rules" in Christianity (written on our hearts, not paper or stone), but many things are dependent on the person themself. Sin can be anything that may destroy that person; therefore, it can be almost anything that disturbs that individual's psyche: a television set in the house, fishing on Sunday, watching movies, or eating and/or drinking something many other people find no biblical objection to. Notice again what the Apostle Paul says in verses 14:14 and 20-22.

Note that the latter part of verse 22, he says, "Blessed are those who don't feel guilty for doing something they have decided is right." So, it is okay to do it if you know it is not forbidden in scripture and your conscience doesn't forbid it. You do not have to give it up because you know of other people that think it is a sin. You just don't insult their faith by doing it in their presence or arguing with them about it. If you think they are being overly zealous in restricting their self, pray for God to reveal that to them. A Paul warns us, picking arguments over it may destroy the person's faith.

Scriptures used to explain personal conviction can, in and of themselves, be misused. Therefore, do not be a "categorizer" by analyzing these verses, categorizing them, sanitizing them and then putting a burden on yourself (and others) that even the Pharisees probably couldn't bear. If you try to please everyone who has "weak" Christian belief issues, you'll drive yourself and family crazy. No matter what you do to try to not offend them, in case they "catch" you, you can't go far enough! There will always be someone who has a religious conviction somewhere that condemns you no matter what you do. Just be at peace with God and avoid situations when you can. Remember what Paul said in Romans 14:22 we just looked at, "Blessed are those who don't feel guilty for doing something they have decided is right." We are Blessed, don't turn personal conviction into a curse. But as Paul says, "But if you have doubts about whether or not you should eat something, you are sinning if you go ahead and do it." He is talking about conviction, not worrying about the Smith's seeing you eat those Mosaic Law forbidden oysters! Again, that is a personal thing, not a doctrinal rule.

Doctrine, like rules, should be kept to the KISS Principle–Keep It Short and Simple or some say, "Keep It Short Stupid." I prefer the former. The Nicene and Apostles' Creeds do an excellent job of stating those precepts essential to the integrity and soundness of the Christian faith. Again, be careful of anything beyond those essentials.

Chapter Eleven

WHAT THE CHURCH OF JESUS CHRIST IS AND IS NOT

—⟨ℰℓℰℓℰ⟩—

The Trap of Tradition: Glue of Culture or Enslaving Chains

Have you ever watched the old movie "Fiddler on the Roof" or seen the play? The one thing that most people remember about it is when the father, Tevye, sings the song about "Tradition!" At the beginning of the story, he is big believer in the Jewish and "hometown" traditions of his little village in Russia. He has a number of daughters and wants all of them to go through the traditional matchmaking and marry the men the family and the matchmaker chooses for them. But times are changing and, fortunately, Tevye has a big heart for his daughters and changes, too. He is able to weather the changes, just barely, but because he learns to change he does better than many others when the changes become more severe including government persecution.

The Dangers of Traditionalism

> "Neither a wise man nor a brave man lies down on the tracks of
> history to wait for the train of the future to run over him." – Dwight
> D. Eisenhower

So said General and later President Eisenhower, but in almost every major war in human history initially there are unnecessarily horrendous losses of life because of unhealthy adherences to outdated traditions in warfare tactics. In the American Colonial era, British troops (and unfortunately some of ours commanded by British trained commanders) would stand in tight formations in open fields and exchange fire with opposing troops, only yards away, firing muskets and cannon at them. It was suicidal, but that was the "traditional" way of doing it at the time. It was the "fair" way of fighting! When American troops, not British trained, hid behind rocks and trees and shot at the British troops with rifles instead of muskets (much more accurate and a lot less stupid) they were labeled as terrorists for not fighting "fair."

In the beginning stages of World War I, the English lost almost an entire generation of college graduates and college men. (By the way, I am not picking on my British friends!) Why this group? Because these were the obvious candidates for officers and officers charged the enemy—on foot or horseback—at the forward point of their troops, leading them into battle. Problem was that machine guns, particularly water cooled ones that could fire for a long time, clouds of poisonous gases and other horribly efficient killing methods had become primary weapons of choice and, as a result, almost an entire generation of young men destined to be the new political and business leaders of England was slaughtered needlessly because of "traditional thinking." J. R. R. Tolkien (*Lord of the Rings*) was a survivor of these outdated tactics and many believe that the horrible, desolate battlegrounds of his books are a reflection of that experience. If you have seen the movie "War Horse" those scenes are accurate of what WWI was like.

With the approach of World War II, the French, leaning on historical methods of defensive fighting, built a line of fortifications between French soil and the Germans. For politically correct reasons they could not extend this Maginot Line along the Belgian border since they had declared neutrality in any conflict. They neglected to notice that rapid mobility and airpower were the new dynamics of warfare and the Germans had a nasty habit of ignoring neutrality. The Germans merely rushed their mobilized armies through Belgium into France or flew over the fortifications, laid siege to the fortifications or ignored them and began their conquests.

People hate change and traditions help shield them from the pains of change. But holding on to outdated traditions can be fatal for individuals and churches. "Dead" churches are usually holding onto outdated traditions as if they are the "will of God" and not really their fears about tomorrow. If we follow the Apostle Paul's advice we'd be better off. After explaining to the Corinthians that God will take care of them if they will look to Him, he tells them, "[33] Instead, desire first and foremost God's kingdom and God's righteousness, and all these things will be given to you as well. [34] Therefore, stop worrying about tomorrow, because tomorrow will worry about itself. Each day has enough trouble of its own" (Matthew 6:33-34, CEB). It is not a "Pollyanna" declaration–"each day has enough trouble of its own"–but realistic.

This is good straight forward and honest advice. Things do ultimately change and with change often comes trouble. I like what a well-known Texas evangelist is known for saying about Christians whining over trouble, "Get over it!" Life changes and if we try to hang on to traditions that are no longer valid or even have become toxic, we'll pay the price! Church congregations will pay a higher price–dwindling membership and a lack of spiritual life in the congregation. If not careful, they will eventually slip into the strangling bonds of legalism and become a "dead" church.

> "Traditionalists are pessimists about the future and optimists about
> the past."–Lewis Mumford

Mumford's statement is amusing and somewhat true in that "traditionalists" are often the problem, not tradition itself. There are many good traditions that give a family, a city, a denomination, a church congregation, or a nation some-thing to hold onto in times of troubles. But supporters of traditions should never be blinded by their devotion to their traditions. As already mentioned, blind traditions (mounted cavalry charging entrenched enemy positions with a high volume of firepower circa WWI) can lead to ruin and failure and in war have cost nations innumerable young lives. The traditionalist that Mumford describes is the one always looking back and never forward, or even in the present. Living in the past does not meet our contemporary needs. The past is dead and living in the past leads to "deadness" in our Christian walk.

The Dangers of Relevancy

There is also the problem of going too far to the other extreme and "throwing the baby out with the wash water." Some churches in seeking to be relevant to the contemporary culture around them become "traditionally anti-traditional." Traditionally here having the same definition as "group think" or "corporate mentality." They try so hard to be culturally relevant that they are in danger of becoming spiritually irrelevant. Words like "tradition" or "structure" become the bad words to be totally avoided except in a negative connotation. Like some of the churches addressed in the Book of Revelation, their focus is diverted away from Jesus Christ. A.W. Tozer, in 1948, noticed this trend in American churches. In his famous book, *The Pursuit of God* he states, "To great sections of the Church the art of worship has been lost entirely, and in its place has come that strange and foreign thing called the "program." This word has been borrowed from the stage and applied with sad wisdom to the type of public service which now passes for worship among us."[xxvii]

A.W. Tozer is known for his book *The Pursuit of God* in which he directs people back to the essentials of Christianity. He well knew and taught that real Christian worship and living comes from the Spirit of God and not man-developed programs. As he stated, before television came into being, the idea of programming came from the entertainment industry. How to get and keep people's attention through human means is what a program is. Do we need some structure, some format to our church meetings? Of course we do; but we must never let it get in the way of God's desires and actions. We need to be ready to forgo them when the Spirit of God starts to move and we need to be ever ready to allow Him to be in charge. Which means, like tradition, format for church services should not ever be "chiseled in stone."

The real Jesus, and people focused on Him, not the rules of legalism or cultural relevancy, is all the attractant necessary to draw crowds as evidenced in the great spiritual awakenings of our own American history. Both groups have totally missed the boat and I, long ago, had quite enough and jumped out of the boat into the turbulent but satisfying "Sea of Non-Religion" (also called the "River of Life"). The sea turned out to be more peaceful than the boat. I might drown, but the Holy Spirit buoys me up. And the water is warm and comforting unlike the anxiety, or apathy, or frenzied activities or even open rebelliousness on the boat.

If it was Good Enough for Grandpa!

"We would rather be ruined than changed,
We would rather die in our dread
Than climb the cross of the moment
And let our illusions die." — W. H. Auden

Mr. Auden does a good job of visually describing the doctrinal stubbornness that robs so many Christians of a more fulfilling relationship with the Lord. How many times have you run across the "if it was good enough for grandpa, it's good enough for me (or you)" mentality? A Christian friend of mine was a member of a small church in East Texas (what we Texans call "deep East Texas") as a young man. They did not have an indoor toilet. Members and visitors had to use an outhouse. (If you don't know what that is, look it up.) I had to use one when I was a kid (at night with a flashlight, it was really scary!) and literally, I thank God for indoor plumbing! It was black widow spiders, centipedes and poisonous snakes we worried about then. We didn't even know about brown recluse spiders which those old wooden outhouses were probably full of.

He and some friends saw the problem with non-returning visitors, or the lack thereof, and proposed to the pastor turning an unused room into an indoor restroom. They had drawn up the plans and were ready to get right to it. The third-generation pastor's reply, "If the outhouse was good enough for my father and his father's church, it is good enough for people now." Nix to indoor facilities. Tradition ruled. They had very few repeat visitors needless to say! (To be honest, with refusal to provide adequate modern toilet facilities for visitors and the congregation, there were probably some serious doctrinal issues as well.)

Tradition can be the glue that holds a group or culture together, but it can also easily become the chains that prevent that group from developing or growing into what God wants them to be. Change is hard; people don't like it. They resist it, but change is inevitable. The social culture of the 1930s and 40s is very different from now, but that is where some church groups want to stay (and die) even today in the 21st century. It often is not intentional. Their church service format is what they grew up in. Their parents had carried that church culture forward several decades. It is a "family thing." I've visited and even been a member of such churches. (The church my wife and I attend now fought to get out of that spiritually stymying mode and did! Praise God!)

Those who are hanging on to the past want to sing the "old songs" but often for the wrong reasons. At one time those songs had power, but instead have usually only become icons sung without any power to remind them of a bygone church era and period in their life. If the song is used to actually praise God and helps the worshiper to worship God, it is good no matter how old or new! Some songs may remind us of church history. My favorites among the "old" songs are those that remind us of the Holiness of God. All this is good, but the participant must be worshipping God through the use of the song, or *it is only a song, it is not worship, it is a "sing along!"* (Some contemporary artists are bringing many old hymns back into use by updating the music some and tuning them more toward dynamic worship and praise once again.)

During the Charismatic Renewal of the '70s, I would often hear the biting comments from unthinking older church members that the new songs being sung were just "silly ditties." Those "ditties" were usually holy scripture, especially psalms, set to music and sung to glorify God! But in their bitterness toward change (and the church coming back to life) these individuals were literally insulting the Word by belittling scripture from being sung to glorify God. (Which is what David, the shepherd/king wrote the Psalms for!) It also showed their loss of knowledge of Bible content from becoming complacent in the reading of the Word. This kind of criticism is something any of us (and we probably have) can be guilty of, if we are not careful, so we need to think before criticizing. As a Christian, we have no business being critical anyway.

> Sometimes it's good to put the paddle down and just let the canoe glide.[xxviii] – Simon Mainwaring

But most people simply can't let go of that "paddle" no matter how tired they are and how the current is immutably moving them forward. The "current" of the Holy Spirit is a gentle current! If people would just let the Holy Spirit guide them through change and legitimate troubled times, they wouldn't wear themselves out fighting it or trying to negotiate rapids on their own. Those who can't put the paddle down are usually at a loss as to why no "younger" people come to visit their church or stay after visiting. There are two extremes I've experienced: the church where all the older saints have left and those where you only see white, grey, and no hair. Both are symptoms of handling change in the human way, not God's way. A "Jesus" church is multi-generational.

> "I'll go anywhere as long as it's forward." – David Livingstone

Now, that's the attitude to have when it comes to change. Think about the challenges that David Livingston undertook to evangelize a largely unexplored (by Europeans) continent. Many of the old hymns promoted this zest for evangelism, but succumbed eventually to being merely "popular" or, sadly, just Hymn 304 in the hymn book. (Nothing wrong with hymn books, by the way.)

The wrong is just the "categorized" and "euthanized" attitude that can develop about the contents, but that can happen even when they are projected onto a screen in the church. The song should always be a vessel for us to worship God, to "keep our eyes on Jesus."

The particular song is not important, our relationship and praise of Jesus is! Worship and praise should not be separate concepts in a congregation's approach to relating to God! Worship is praise to God. It can be with musical instruments, a cappella (without instruments), or in many styles, as long as it helps us enter into a praising attitude in singing to the Lord. It can be a song, a chant, or just recitation as long as it is enabling us to praise God. Even in prayer, if we are tuned in we are worshipping God while we talk to Him. Praise comes from the "heart" not the lungs.

Music styles change in only a few decades (or less), but God's principles do not! Unfortunately, people identify the cultural issues of their growth period with God's principles. Two different things! In the field of International Relations, this is called "ethnocentrism" which basically means, "If it ain't my way, it's no way!" Of all people, Christians should know better. We have "Westernized" a Middle Eastern creed and think everyone should have services and think the same way we do!

Real worship isn't an hour to an hour and one-half of recitation, songs, choir, and upbeat sermons ending just in time to beat the other churches to the restaurants or to get home for the football game on television. Real worship has no time limits; real worship even has no human leader, except as directed by the Holy Spirit. We need to quit being so hung up on how we or our parents did it and pay more attention to what church is really about. It's about honing our relationship to God, not entertainment, not programs, not "singing the old songs" because they make us comfortable, not being anti-traditionally culturally relevant or hardcore traditional. Let's get back to what it is really intended to be about–loving on our Loving God!

Every generation, not just the one you may have dealt with, if you are already a Christian, had its own cherished and/or comfortable things it doesn't want to let go of and, if not careful, becomes the next group of "traditionalists" resisting the changes necessary for the church to remain healthy. They, unintentionally, become the mockers of the next move of God in the Church of Jesus Christ. Again, we should not strive to be "relevant", but we need to be flexible as the culture changes. Our striving to improve ourselves or our ministries or our congregations needs to be by the Holy Spirit's guidance and encouragement to study the Word, to pray, to seek communion with God. The striving we don't need in the church is the human effort which we tend to transfer from the workplace to the prayer place, when it should be the other way around.

When the Apostle Paul was preaching to the Jews at the synagogue in Antioch of Pisidia, he warned them:

> [38] Therefore, my friends, I want you to know that through Jesus the forgiveness of sins is proclaimed to you. [39] Through him everyone who believes is set free from every sin, a justification you were not able to obtain under the law of Moses. [40] Take care that what the prophets have said does not happen to you:[41] "Look, you scoffers, wonder and perish, for I am going to do something in your days that you would never believe, even if someone told you" (Acts 13:38-41, NIV).

Don't be the future scoffer when you "age" because you don't like change. It doesn't take reading much scripture to realize that God does not like the act of scoffing!

The Sin of the Pharisees and Sadducees (or Don't Be Caught Trying to Hold Back the New Covenant Church!)

The "fullness of time" had finally come. In his letter to the Galatian Church, Paul said, "[4] But when the fullness [sic] of the time was come, God sent forth his Son, made of a woman, made under the law, [5] To redeem them that were under the law, that we might receive the adoption of sons (Galatians 4:4-5, KJV). The King James has a more beautiful way of saying it, but it in more contemporary language it is said, "⁴ But when the right time came, God sent his Son, born of a woman, subject to the law. ⁵ God sent him to buy freedom for us who were slaves to the law, so that he could adopt us as his very own children" (Galatians 4:4-5, NLT). "The right time came" is clearer, but doesn't have the "depth" of "fullness of time."

The "church" was about to change dramatically with Jesus prophecied arrival. The Promise would be fulfilled and the Law no longer needed as a tutor for believers. It would be replaced by the Christ, the Messiah and by spiritual insight and guidance by God's own Holy Spirit. There would be "open membership!" But there were people in authority that refused to accept the change. It wasn't just power and fear of change, it was fear of very bloody reprisals by the Roman army if the Romans sensed the people considering rising up to create a new non-Roman kingdom because of a new charismatic Jewish leader. They didn't understand that Jesus had not come to lead a revolt to establish a new political entity but to establish the New Covenant Church.

The only people Jesus was outwardly antagonistic to were the Pharisees and Sadducees, the so-called religious experts (and mockers) of their day. These men, with their knowledge and learning, should have known Him as the Messiah, but they didn't or refused to believe that the promised Redeemer had finally come. Luke, the author of Acts relates what happened in one instance in the book of Acts when the Pharisees once again demanded a sign of who He really was,

[16] The Pharisees and Sadducees came to Jesus and tested him by asking him to show them a sign from heaven.
[2] He replied, "When evening comes, you say, 'It will be fair weather, for the sky is red,' [3] and in the morning, 'Today it will be stormy, for the sky is red and overcast.' You know how to interpret the appearance of the sky, but you cannot interpret the signs of the times (Matthew 16:1-3, NIV).

In other words, there were plenty of signs all over the place, many of them fulfilling prophecies that the Pharisees and Sadducees knew by heart. Greed, power, fear of the Romans, there were all kinds of human reasons that they refused to see what was right in front of them. How many people today, us included, do the same thing when it comes to God's evidences? They are all around us as Paul said in his Roman letter, "[20] For the invisible things of him from the creation of the world are clearly seen, being understood by the things that are made, even his eternal power and Godhead; so that they are without excuse..." (Romans 1:20, KJV). The night sky was once a great testimony of this until it was light polluted to the point anyone living near a city cannot see it anymore. To see the beauty of nature is something very few modern people get to do. When they do go "outdoors" many have such an intense agenda of "enjoying the out-of-doors" that they miss it all!

There were some religious leaders who believed in Jesus and knew He was from God, at least a prophet and, to some, probably the Messiah. But they were afraid to speak out publicly. The Apostle John tells us about one of these secret believers, "3 "There was a Pharisee named Nicodemus, a Jewish leader. [2] He came to Jesus at night and said to him, "Rabbi, we know that you are a teacher who has come from God, for no one could do these miraculous signs that you do unless God is with him."

[3] Jesus answered, "I assure you, unless someone is born anew, it's not possible to see God's kingdom" (John 3:1-3, CEB).

Despite some of the religious leaders "knowing" who Jesus was and that with the coming of the Messiah, prophecies would be fulfilled that would change their religious world forever, they tenaciously held on to their Old Covenant (think church) traditions:

Jesus Teaches about Inner Purity

15 Some Pharisees and teachers of religious law now arrived from Jerusalem to see Jesus. They asked him, [2] "Why do your

disciples disobey our age-old tradition? For they ignore our tradition of ceremonial hand washing before they eat."

[3] Jesus replied, "And why do you, by your traditions, violate the direct commandments of God? [4] For instance, God says, 'Honor your father and mother,' and 'Anyone who speaks disrespectfully of father or mother must be put to death.' [5] But you say it is all right for people to say to their parents, 'Sorry, I can't help you. For I have vowed to give to God what I would have given to you.' [6] In this way, you say they don't need to honor their parents. And so you cancel the word of God for the sake of your own tradition. [7] You hypocrites! Isaiah was right when he prophesied about you, for he wrote,

[8] 'These people honor me with their lips, but their hearts are far from me. [9] Their worship is a farce, for they teach man-made ideas as commands from God'" (Matthew 15:1-9, NLT).

As the religious types berated Jesus for not following their man-created laws and rituals which had become more important to them than God's love, He returned a "broadside" based upon one of their most grievous creations–a law that diverted money into the Temple treasury that should have been going to elderly or handicapped parents! This "law" allowed someone to be "blessed" for violating one of the Ten Commandments–honor your mother and father.

We need to review our "traditions" once in a while to make sure we are not holding back cultural changes that are being directed by God for the health and growth of His Church, not ours. If these religious leaders had been less hung up on their traditions (and avarice in some cases) and more lead by God, they would have read the "times" and known who Jesus was and why He was there. But, realistically, this was prophetically meant to be. God knew it would happen and He would have to send His Son to pay the price for this very attitude on mankind's part.

Mankind has a nasty habit of looking the other way when they should be looking at God. Even the scriptures can be misused in this way. The Apostle John said, "[39]"You search the Scriptures because you think they give you eternal life. But the Scriptures point to me! [40] Yet you refuse to come to me to receive this life.

[41] "Your approval means nothing to me, [42] because I know you don't have God's love within you. [43] For I have come to you in my Father's name, and you have rejected me. Yet if others come in their own name, you gladly welcome them" (John 5:39-43, NLT).

This is a trap that any Christian group can fall into! Many people get hung up on the Word itself, but it is only a guidebook to Jesus, the true Word. A. W. Tozer from the mid-20th century said it this way, "The Bible is not an end in itself, but a means to bring men to an intimate and satisfying knowledge of God, that they may enter into Him, that they may delight in His presence, may taste and know the inner sweetness of the very God Himself in the core and center of their hearts."[xxviii]

Jesus predates the written Word and is the Word Himself according to John:

Prologue: Christ, the Eternal Word
1 "In the beginning the Word already existed.
The Word was with God,
and the Word was God.
[2] He existed in the beginning with God.
[3] God created everything through him,
and nothing was created except through him.
[4] The Word gave life to everything that was created,
and his life brought light to everyone.
[5] The light shines in the darkness,
and the darkness can never extinguish it" (John 1:1-5, NLT).

In the Pharisee's time, they only had the Old Testament (and a whole bunch of extra rules they made up), but it contained an abundance of prophecies predicting Jesus coming. Now, we have the New Testament with inspired records of Jesus and the early church. We, also, have the active work of the Holy Spirit. The problem is that people become so entranced with the written word and how they can follow it, that they forget that they are supposed to be reading the Word in order to follow Jesus. They take their eyes off God and put them on ink and paper. How ridiculous would you look if you bought a brand new appliance or machine that you really wanted and all you did was leave it in the carton and read the instruction manual, praising its (the manual) virtues, but never open the box? I can picture a guy sitting by a crate containing a brand new Harley-Davidson motorcycle that he has been given, but all he does is read the manual that came with it. Pretty ridiculous, right? But that is what a lot of us do with Jesus! (It's safer?)

A Wake up Call for Modern Churches from the "Ancient" Book of Revelation

There are all kinds of ways that men and women pervert the Word of God to suit themselves, to enslave others, or to make life more unbearable than it already can be. Some of them are even well meaning. But they are tailoring their (not God's) creation based upon their own sense of guilt and need for punishment or discipline or just a desire to categorize and control. God's Word is meant to make our lives more bearable, not less! It is meant to give us life, not death! It is meant to free us, not enslave us! Freedom, not religious feudalism, is what Jesus brought to us. Many years ago, I came across a saying which I use to this day, "Religion is the way man tries to control God (and people), relationship is what God wants with man." Religion, not legitimate Christianity, has often been used over the centuries to control populations of nations. That is, again, why the USA banned having a state religion. Combine government bureaucrats and a state mandated religious doctrine and you have something more toxic than any EPA Superfund Site.

I believe that we people of Western Civilization have a strong tendency to categorize everything possible. There are some of us who are really bad about this–very analytical. I'm one and have to be very careful. People take the Word of God, analyze it, categorize it, sanitize it, legalize it, and, as a result, euthanize it! It becomes merely dead religion or masses of rules that followers numb their minds and their hearts to God trying to follow in order to please Him by their adherence to, mostly, man-made rules. That is not Christianity! That is man-made religion! It only leads to death. And it can be done with good intentions. Jesus addressed this problem with several churches in the book of Revelation. This is to His Church at Ephesus, a purportedly good church:

> [2] I know all the things you do. I have seen your hard work and
> your patient endurance. I know you don't tolerate evil people. You
> have examined the claims of those who say they are apostles but
> are not. You have discovered they are liars. [3] You have patiently
> suffered for me without quitting. [4] "But I have this complaint
> against you. You don't love me or each other as you did at first! [5]
> Look how far you have fallen! Turn back to me and do the works
> you did at first. If you don't repent, I will come and remove your
> lampstand from its place among the churches. [6] But this is in
> your favor: You hate the evil deeds of the Nicolaitans, just as I
> do (Revelation 2:2-6, NLT).

First, notice that Jesus, the Son of God, practices what more Christians who consider themselves good bosses, managers, or counselors should practice. He has some problems with these folks, but He first tells them what He likes that they are doing! That is good counseling! But then He tells them the problem–they have become hung up on the details and lost their focus of loving Him and each other first, before everything else! They have analyzed, categorized, sanitized, and euthanized His teachings! He warns them that if they don't rectify this, He is going to take away their "golden lampstand." That doesn't sound good.

I think it is safe to say that if they did not put the emphasis back on loving Him and each other, the Church of Ephesus would cease to exist. He did not say they should stop testing prophets or hanging in there under persecution. He said these are important but secondary to number one–love God with all your heart and your neighbor as yourself.

The Primary Mission of a Church

The primary mission of a church body is to worship, praise, and fellowship with God. Second to that is to win souls for the Lord. We don't do that by condemnation or, as some put it, "beating people over the head with a Bible." Jesus provided the avenue and the Holy Spirit the connection. We present the evidence and the Holy Spirit does the convicting, just as we read in scripture earlier. Everything else to do with the functioning of the church comes after these things!

I was a product of the Charismatic Renewal of the 60s and 70s. I had finally read the Bible in my language and was on fire for God. But when we would visit churches, I couldn't understand why they sang *about* Jesus or *about* the church or about a hundred other things, but never sang **to Jesus!** Worship and praise are exactly that! Singing favorite songs week after week that evoke no love for God is not worship. It may be fun, enjoyable, but it is not worship. Again, that is called a "sing along." It is lukewarm Christianity. Here's what Jesus says about lukewarm churches: (Kind of scary!)

The Message to the Church in Laodicea

> [14]Write this letter to the angel of the church in Laodicea. This is the message from the one who is the Amen—the faithful and true witness, the beginning of God's new creation: [15] "I know all the things you do, that you are neither hot nor cold. I wish that you were one or the other! [16] But since you are like lukewarm water, neither hot nor cold, I will spit you out of my mouth! [17] You say, 'I am rich. I have everything I want. I don't need a thing!' And you don't realize that you are wretched and miserable and poor and blind and naked" (Revelation 3:14-17, NLT).

Ever bite into cold, soggy french fries? Ugh! Hot would be good! On fire for Jesus would be great! But what about cold? These are Jesus words to the church at Sardis:

The Message to the Church in Sardis

> 3 "Write this letter to the angel of the church in Sardis. This is the message from the one who has the sevenfold Spirit of God and the seven stars:
>
> "I know all the things you do, and that you have a reputation for being alive—but you are dead. [2] Wake up! Strengthen what little remains, for even what is left is almost dead. I find that your actions do not meet the requirements of my God. [3] Go back to what you heard and believed at first; hold to it firmly. Repent and turn to me again. If you don't wake up, I will come to you suddenly, as unexpected as a thief" (Revelation 3:1-3, NLT).

This letter was to be sent to this church by John the Apostle. Notice in verse two that He says that Sardis has a reputation of being "alive." How many churches who are deemed alive because of their large congregations, music programs, television broadcasts, etc. will find on the Day of Judgment that they were emphasizing the wrong "alive" and will sadly find that they were only popular, not "alive." To be truly alive, the emphasis must be on a personal and corporate relationship to God, not "eyewash." Not "tinsel."

So, what have we learned from reviewing these scriptures? A church must be approachable by the contemporary culture, but not striving to be relevant which can lead to even more problems and a loss of spiritual perspective–like the Church of Laodicea and Sardis in the Book of Revelation. We would all probably shudder to think that God would have the same opinion of our church. Traditions can be good, but when they become all-important and block our view of God's Will, this is a problem. We need to avoid "traditionalism" where church traditions are more important than our connection to Jesus. As leaders, or as members, we need to be very careful about criticism. Not something Jesus likes us doing anyway, but a condemning spirit can develop and blind us to what God is trying to tell us. Even Gamaliel, one of the most reputable teachers of the Pharisees, tried to tell the rest of them this:

> [29] But Peter and the apostles replied, "We must obey God rather than any human authority. [30] The God of our ancestors raised Jesus from the dead after you killed him by hanging him on a cross. [31] Then God put him in the place of honor at his right hand as Prince and Savior. He did this so the people of Israel would repent of their sins and be forgiven. [32] We are witnesses of these things and so is the Holy Spirit, who is given by God to those who obey him."
>
> [33] When they heard this, the high council was furious and decided to kill them. [34] But one member, a Pharisee named Gamaliel, who was an expert in religious law and respected by all the people, stood up and ordered that the men be sent outside the council chamber for a while. [35] Then he said to his colleagues, "Men of Israel, take care what you are planning to do to these men! [36] Some time ago there was that fellow Theudas, who pretended to be someone great. About 400 others joined him, but he was killed, and all his followers went their various ways. The whole movement came to nothing. [37] After him, at the time of the census, there was Judas of Galilee. He got people to follow him, but he was killed, too, and all his followers were scattered.[38] So my advice is, leave these men alone. Let them go. If they are planning and doing these things merely on their own, it will soon be overthrown. [39] But if it is from God, you will not be able to overthrow them. You may even find yourselves fighting against God!" (Acts 5:29-39, NLT)

Fighting against God is not good; but how many of us, as individuals or congregations, are doing just that to one extent or another without realizing it? God says if you love Me you will obey me. How do we measure up to that? This chapter is getting a little long and I promised to follow the KISS principle. So, to finalize this chapter, I would say this:

"Hang on to Jesus" – "The Times They are A'Changin'"

We are now in the age of technology. There are more scientists working on more breakthroughs in technology than ever before in the history of mankind. It is not just sneaky marketing, products really are practically obsolete the minute they hit the shelf. Don't be the "pastor" who snatches cell phones from people thinking they are being rude when they are looking up the scripture you are working from! Society is changing. This affects congregations. Don't be like the religious leaders of Roman Judea trying to hold back the tide. The New Testament/Covenant Church has to hold on to basic doctrine and precepts, but be able to adapt and not become the dying congregations still trying to live in the church culture of the 1940s or 50s.

God's Church is always fresh and never withering, never stale. We need to "Hang onto Jesus" as the old idiom says, but that does not mean a painted (or tainted) "idea" of Jesus in our minds. It means the real Jesus—and, guess what, He is alive and "fresh every morning." We need to be fresh also, not moldering, in the "revered past!" We do that by hanging on to Him in our "hearts" not just our minds!

Chapter Twelve

AGREE TO DISAGREE—IT IS A FREE COUNTRY

—⟨⟩⟨⟩—

Y ears ago I was having a discussion with a pastor who leaned toward the cultural relevancy model, but that I know loves the Lord with all his heart. At that time I leaned a little more toward the more structured model (but not legalistic, I'd had my "legalistic" binge early on). He made the statement that "We can agree to disagree." I agree, but to that I would add today that this is a free country—a nation founded upon freedom of religion due to our Founding Fathers and their ancestor's experiences in Europe with dictators, monarchs and their infernal state churches. State churches that persecuted anyone who: 1) tried to bring the Bible into the common language where people could understand it and realize they were being "bamboozled" by their leaders and 2) tried to worship God outside of the official channels (where they couldn't be monitored). (If you think communism can be bad, try a state controlled church.) Even in the early colonies people had no choice of where to go to church. You went to the official church in your village or could be punished. This was prior to the Great Awakening of the Colonial Era.

Today, in the United States of America, our leadership and our citizens have forgotten how to agree to disagree. We almost seem on the verge of our own "Hundred Years' War" over politics and religion. The politicians play this to their advantage building up voting blocs, often either pro-Christian voting blocs or, these days, anti-Christian (the people they are manipulating don't realize that they are anti-Christian however, so don't condemn them). This is a sad state of affairs. The Christian Church has placed their head in the sand and often allowed only the most radical of our group to be our speakers. It is time for love to reign, not hateful, belligerent rhetoric directed at people doing things they have been deceived into doing.

The entertainment industry, mostly very liberal (which, again, they are entitled to their viewpoints) usually present Christians as stupid, arrogant, elitist, haughty, exploiters, and (the new word) "haters." Oh they love to promote that one right now. Unfortunately, they find models for these terms too easily. The evening news makes it easy with some of the "extremists" we have claiming to be "Christian" arrogantly displaying their mean-spirited media events to bring the media's cameras and commentators.

Christians conquer with love—God's love—not hate or condemnation; not by disturbing grieving families at funerals; or getting more Americans killed or Christians persecuted by being mean-spirited about other religious groups for whom they should be praying instead. Prayer accomplishes a whole lot more than burning another religion's holy book, one that they treat with a lot more respect than the average Christian does his Bible.

Are the politicians following the lead of an intolerant society, or is the citizenry following the bad behavior of the politicians (and the media/entertainment industry)? Wouldn't it be nice if educational circles (down-streamed from Washington, DC) could, instead of pushing various political or social agendas, just focus on civility and courtesy. We have problems in our country, but we still have the best thing going in all of history. Let's not blow it. According to historians, upon Ben Franklin's emergence from the Constitutional Convention in 1787, he was asked what kind of government the new nation now had, to which he answered, "A Republic, if you can keep it."

Perhaps because of civics classes of the past, we became arrogant that we could keep this republic without applying any effort. We spent too much time studying how successful the USA had been up until that point, and assumed it would always be so, but why? Because we didn't explore the *because*, we now live in a non-civil society in which the media and politicians prey on our animosities toward each other (as groups). So what can we as Christians or like-minded folks do about this increasingly dangerous climate?

Jesus said that His followers are the "salt," the preservative of society. We are supposed to be the light on a hill, a beacon. Jesus had this to say to us: "[13] You are the salt of the earth. But what good is salt if it has lost its flavor? Can you make it salty again? It will be thrown out and trampled underfoot as worthless. [14] You are the light of the world—like a city on a hilltop that cannot be hidden. [15] No one lights a lamp and then puts it under a basket. Instead, a lamp is placed on a stand, where it gives light to everyone in the house. [16] In the same way, let your good deeds shine out for all to see, so that everyone will praise your heavenly Father" (Matthew 5:13-16 ,NLT).

I fear that we have been marginalized by a long period (now over) of prosperity and intimidated by contemporary anti-Christian agendas. It is time to stop! We have lost our "saltiness" and hidden the lamp under a basket. We are supposed to lead in establishing Godly principles in our culture whether the people who live in it love God or not. We need to get the good salt of Gaza that does not become tasteless, take that lamp out from under the basket and put it on a stand. We need to light up this culture as our predecessors have before us. Have we forgotten so much?

Later in the Gospel of Matthew, Jesus is quoted as saying, "[44] But I tell you this: Love your enemies, and pray for those who persecute you. [45] In this way you show that you are children of your Father in heaven. He makes his sun rise on people whether they are good or evil. He lets rain fall on them whether they are just or unjust" (Matthew 5:44-45, GW). God pours out His grace on all who will accept it, even if they do not accept Him. Why can't we do the same? Why do we have to be portrayed as being mean-spirited instead of what God destined us to be–love-spirited!

It is time for us to quit being reactionary and become "proactionary." It is time to quit allowing ourselves to be manipulated by politicians and phony

"Christian" leaders. Our leader is the Creator of the world and Jesus became our High Priest so that we don't need someone to stand between us and God, except Him. Let's "quit" the lazy-Christian syndrome and be known for our good deeds and love for our fellow man–Christian or not! As Christians, let's be the first to "agree to disagree" and be the example–the salt and the light which Jesus intended for us to be! It is not about just getting to go to Heaven, it is about taking a host of people with us–would you deny them that?

ENDNOTES

i.   The Online Library of Liberty, http://oll.libertyfund.org/index.php?option=com_staticxt&staticfile=advanced_search.php

ii.   Ibid.

iii.   © 2003 by Kenneth L. Weatherford. All rights reserved.

iv.   Tozer, A.W.; Tozer, Aidan; Tozer, Aidan Wilson (2011-01-31). The Pursuit of God by A.W. Tozer (Special Kindle Enabled Edition with Interactive Table of Contents and Built in Text-to-Speech Features) (Illustrated) ... | The Writings of Aiden Wilson Tozer of) (Kindle Locations 709-714). Christian Miracle Foundation Press. Kindle Edition.

v.   Tozer, A.W.; Tozer, Aidan; Tozer, Aidan Wilson (2011-01-31). The Pursuit of God by A.W. Tozer (Special Kindle Enabled Edition with Interactive Table of Contents and Built in Text-to-Speech Features) (Illustrated) ... | The Writings of Aiden Wilson Tozer of) (Kindle Locations 1021-1026). Christian Miracle Foundation Press. Kindle Edition.

vi.   Rosalie June Slater, Noah Webster: Founding Father of Scholarship and Education, in Noah Webster's An American Dictionary of the English Language, Facsimile First Edition. Chesapeake, VA: Foundation for American Christian Education (www.face.net), 1967, 11.

vii.   Ibid

viii.   Ibid

ix.   Juli Camarin, http://www.jcblog.net/, "Jesus Was Tempted In Every Way, Yet Without Sin (Hebrews 4:15)" USA, Nov 30, 2010.

x.   http://dictionary.reference.com/browse/sin

xi.   Tozer, A.W.; Tozer, Aidan; Tozer, Aidan Wilson (2011-01-31). The Pursuit of God by A.W. Tozer (Special Kindle Enabled Edition with Interactive Table of Contents and Built in Text to Speech Features) (Illustrated) ... | The Writings of Aiden Wilson Tozer of) (Kindle Locations 1056-1057). Christian Miracle Foundation Press. Kindle Edition.

xii.   (http://www.messagebible.com) copyright information.

xiii. Tozer, A.W.; Tozer, Aidan; Tozer, Aidan Wilson (2011-01-31). The Pursuit of God by A.W. Tozer (Special Kindle Enabled Edition with Interactive Table of Contents and Built in Text to Speech Features) (Illustrated) ... | The Writings of Aiden Wilson Tozer of) (Kindle Locations 1125-1128). Christian Miracle Foundation Press. Kindle Edition.

xiv.   http://christianity.about.com/od/glossary/a/Agape.htm

xv.   Tozer, A.W.; Tozer, Aidan; Tozer, Aidan Wilson (2011-01-31). The Pursuit of God by A.W. Tozer (Special Kindle Enabled Edition with Interactive Table of Contents and Built in Text to Speech Features) (Illustrated) ... | The Writings of Aiden Wilson Tozer of) (Kindle Locations 194-196). Christian Miracle Foundation Press. Kindle Edition.

xvi.   http://en.wikipedia.org/wiki/Id,_ego,_and_super-ego

xvii. Bruxy Cavey. The End of Religion: Encountering the Subversive Spirituality of Jesus (pp. 34-35). Kindle Edition.

xviii. Tozer, A.W.; Tozer, Aidan; Tozer, Aidan Wilson (2011-01-31). The Pursuit of God by A.W. Tozer (Special Kindle Enabled Edition with Interactive Table of Contents and Built in Text to Speech Features) (Illustrated) ... | The Writings of Aiden Wilson Tozer of) (Kindle Locations 185-189). Christian Miracle Foundation Press. Kindle Edition.

xix.   Dictionary.com.

xx.   Ken Collins, "The Apocrypha and the Old Testament," http://www.kencollins.com/bible/bible-p1.htm#what, Accessed on May 9, 2013, used with permission.

xxi.   Ibid

xxii. Ibid

xxiii. "Greatsite.com" http://www.greatsite.com/timeline-english-bible-history/

xxiv. http://www.thefreedictionary.com/church+doctrine

xxv. http://www.audioenglish.net/dictionary/church_doctrine.htm

xxvi. Tozer, A.W.; Tozer, Aidan; Tozer, Aidan Wilson (2011-01-31). The Pursuit of God by A.W. Tozer (Special Kindle Enabled Edition with Interactive Table of Contents and Built in Text to Speech Features) (Illustrated) ... I The Writings of Aiden Wilson Tozer of) (Kindle Locations 89-91). Christian Miracle Foundation Press. Kindle Edition.

xxvii. http://www.brainyquote.com/quotes/quotes/s/simonmainw493962.html#q6BD6ruF7J9dEbJg.99.

xxviii. Tozer, A.W.; Tozer, Aidan; Tozer, Aidan Wilson (2011-01-31). The Pursuit of God by A.W. Tozer (Special Kindle Enabled Edition with Interactive Table of Contents and Built in Text to Speech Features) (Illustrated) ... I The Writings of Aiden Wilson Tozer of) (Kindle Locations 95-97). Christian Miracle Foundation Press. Kindle Edition.